Rock and Water Gardens

Other Publications:

THE GOOD COOK

THE SEAFARERS

THE ENCYCLOPEDIA OF COLLECTIBLES

THE GREAT CITIES

WORLD WAR II

HOME REPAIR AND IMPROVEMENT

THE WORLD'S WILD PLACES

THE TIME-LIFE LIBRARY OF BOATING

HUMAN BEHAVIOR

THE ART OF SEWING

THE OLD WEST

THE EMERGENCE OF MAN

THE AMERICAN WILDERNESS

LIFE LIBRARY OF PHOTOGRAPHY

THIS FABULOUS CENTURY

FOODS OF THE WORLD

TIME-LIFE LIBRARY OF AMERICA

TIME-LIFE LIBRARY OF ART

GREAT AGES OF MAN

LIFE SCIENCE LIBRARY

THE LIFE HISTORY OF THE UNITED STATES

TIME READING PROGRAM

LIFE NATURE LIBRARY

LIFE WORLD LIBRARY

FAMILY LIBRARY:
    HOW THINGS WORK IN YOUR HOME
    THE TIME-LIFE BOOK OF THE FAMILY CAR
    THE TIME-LIFE FAMILY LEGAL GUIDE
    THE TIME-LIFE BOOK OF FAMILY FINANCE

Rock and Water Gardens

by
OGDEN TANNER
and
the Editors of TIME-LIFE BOOKS

TIME-LIFE BOOKS, ALEXANDRIA, VIRGINIA

THE AUTHOR: Ogden Tanner, a former staff member of TIME-LIFE BOOKS, is
the author of *Garden Construction* and co-author of *Herbs* in The TIME-LIFE Encyclopedia of Gardening. He has also written or edited books on natural history,
science and photography. An architectural graduate of Princeton University, he
has been associate editor of *House & Home* and assistant managing editor of
Architectural Forum.

CONSULTANTS: James Underwood Crockett, author of 13 of the volumes in the
Encyclopedia, co-author of two additional volumes and consultant on other books
in the series, has been a lover of the earth and its good things since his boyhood on
a Massachusetts fruit farm. He was graduated from the Stockbridge School of
Agriculture of the University of Massachusetts and has worked ever since in
horticulture. A perennial contributor to leading gardening magazines, he also
writes a monthly bulletin, "Flowery Talks," that is widely distributed through
retail florists. His television program, *Crockett's Victory Garden,* shown all over
the United States, has won countless converts to the Crockett approach to growing
things. Dr. Robert L. Baker is Associate Professor of Horticulture at the University of Maryland, College Park. H. Lincoln Foster, a past president of the American
Rock Garden Society, wrote the book *Rock Gardening.* Patrick Nutt is a specialist
in aquatic plants at Longwood Gardens, Kennett Square, Pa. Dr. William Louis
Stern is Professor of Botany at the University of Maryland, College Park.

THE COVER: A rock-and-water garden, partially shaded by a Japanese black pine
(left), provides a soothing retreat from the noonday sun. The pool, built on two
levels to create a series of small rippling waterfalls, is equipped with a pump to
recirculate the water. Primroses, grape hyacinths, English daisies and azaleas
nestle among the moss-covered rocks that line the pool's shore, while waterlilies
and a water hawthorn float atop the pool itself.

CONTENTS

Gardens shaped with the earth's basic elements 1

There is something about the idea of rocks and water in a garden that has an irresistible appeal. Partly it is the images they conjure up of mountain peaks and alpine meadows, of boulder-strewn streams and azure lakes. Rocks and water are the basic elements of nature's most stunning and memorable landscapes, and in a garden they supply, even in abbreviated form, a sense of nature's original plan. A well-placed rock or two can suggest the structural bones of the earth, solid, immutable, heaved and shaped by ancient geological forces. Water, their opposite, is quick, vital, changeable. In motion, it bemuses the eye and ear, blotting out other distractions. At rest, it brings the sky down to earth in its reflective surface and hints of dark mysteries within its depths.

But the presence of rocks and water do more for the garden scene than enlarge its spiritual dimensions. Rocks and water also open up a whole new world of plants that are ideally suited to the limited scale of the average suburban lot. An arrangement of rocks designed to simulate a mountain meadow gives the gardener a chance to experiment with alpine shrubs and wildflowers that normally grow above the tree line, where climatic conditions have kept the plants low and compact—without any sacrifice of the beauty of their flowers. In the same space that is customarily occupied by a dozen standard-sized garden specimens, one can grow as many as 40 or 50 alpine plants. And if the tiny alpine species are tucked into the crevices of a stone wall, the space they occupy in the garden is even smaller. Indeed, no other kind of garden offers the possibility of growing more plants of more different descriptions in so small an area.

If water is introduced into the picture, the range of plant materials broadens even further. Aquatic species like waterlilies, lotus and water poppies, which grow in water and nowhere else, are available to the gardener, and so are plants like Japanese irises,

Tucked among sandstone rocks and lava, flowering succulents brighten a hot, dry California slope. Their shallow roots and water-storing leaves make succulents excellent plants for dry rock gardens.

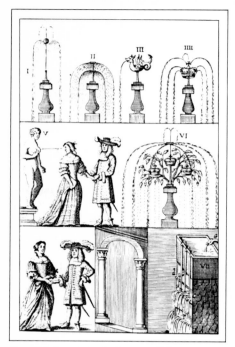

Garden-fountain designers of the 16th and 17th Centuries were marvelously ingenious—though anything but subtle. Many elaborate spraying fountains were built, including an artificial tree with dripping leaves (center, right) and a wall waterfall viewed through an arch (bottom). A favorite was the joke fountain (center, left). Elizabeth I installed a joke fountain in her gardens at Hampton Court to "play upon the ladies and others standing by and give them a thorough wetting."

arrowheads and cattails, which favor a wet, boggy soil. A beginner can start by planting pygmy waterlilies in a wooden tub and, as his skill and interest grow, may progress to more elaborate and permanent designs built into the framework of the garden itself.

An added attraction of rock and water gardens is that, with modern techniques and equipment, they generally require minimal upkeep. In the beginning, of course, there is a certain investment of time, labor and materials to get started. But once functioning, such a garden needs very little pruning, fertilizing, watering or pest control. The major concerns are providing winter protection in cold climates, a good cleanup in spring and fall and a certain amount of weeding to keep things neat.

Although rock and water gardens are now within the reach of everyone, even people in the most modest circumstances, when the design concepts used in creating such gardens were worked out hundreds and even thousands of years ago, rock and water gardens were almost exclusively the province of the nobility. In the ancient civilizations that sprang up along great rivers like the Euphrates and the Nile, water was so central to existence itself, as irrigation for the fields, that it soon became a major motif in landscaping. Gardens from Egypt to India were graced by pools that were both reservoirs and decorative devices in which the sacred lotus often bloomed. Persian noblemen retreated from the desert heat into private walled gardens where flowers bloomed and fountains splashed. And in the earliest gardens of the Orient, cherished by emperors and poets, the natural landscape was evoked in stylized compositions that always included pools, as well as streams, rocks and mounds of earth surmounted by gnarled dwarf trees.

During the Middle Ages, Moorish Spain, drawing on Persian tradition, became famous for its courtyard gardens like those of the Alhambra and Generalife, where water from arching fountains spilled into catch basins and flowed through geometric channels symbolizing the rivers of life. During the Renaissance in Italy, the hillside villas of wealthy noblemen were adorned with grottoes and sculptured fountains; in one instance elaborate waterworks were kept constantly at play by diverting a river. This extravagance was soon imported into the rest of Europe and culminated in the gardens of Versailles, created for Louis XIV, where water mills and pumping machines tapped the Seine and drained the water table for miles around to feed the 1,400 fountain jets and fill the great axial canals on which the Sun King staged mock sea battles for his royal guests, using ships adorned with gold and silver rigging.

The introduction of water into European gardens naturally

brought the cultivation of aquatic plants. A small white waterlily native to Europe, *Nymphaea alba,* was grown in the pools of aristocrats. Late in the 18th Century, a sweet-scented North American species, the New England pond lily, became popular among British gardeners. But it was not until the 19th Century that discoveries abroad and at home made waterlilies and other aquatics international favorites.

On New Year's Day, 1837, Robert Schomburgk, on expedition for the Royal Geographic Society of Great Britain, was traveling the Berbice River in British Guiana. As his party reached a place where the river widened into a lakelike expanse of still water, it came upon an amazing sight: a flotilla of gargantuan plants with floating leaves, each 6 feet or more across with an upturned edge that made it resemble a gigantic platter. Enormous flowers, up to 15 inches in diameter, opened at dusk to release an intoxicating fragrance like that of crushed pineapple. The plants were unlike any Schomburgk had ever seen. The flowers, which first appeared creamy white, changed color almost as he watched. On successive evenings they passed from white to light pink to darker rose; before closing at sunrise on the third morning, they became a glowing purplish-red.

Schomburgk excitedly sent seeds of this vegetable wonder, as he termed it, back to England, where horticulturists tried to make them germinate. It was not until 1849, however, that Joseph Paxton, superintendent of the Duke of Devonshire's gardens at Chatsworth, was able to bring a plant into flower in the Duke's lavish hothouse pools. This event created a sensation and was celebrated with an elaborate entertainment during which Paxton's daughter, dressed as a fairy, was set afloat on one of the huge leaves.

The plant, named *Victoria regia* in honor of England's queen, became so famous that portfolios of Victorian illustrations rarely failed to include a picture of a child in a sunbonnet, sitting demurely on a Victoria leaf. But exacting requirements limited the plant to the estates of wealthy Britons and the Royal Botanic Gardens at Kew. The giant needed a basin 30 feet across and 6 feet deep, generous amounts of fertilizer, lots of sunlight and a water temperature of 80°. Nevertheless, the Queen's lily stimulated European interest in water gardening, including the growing of smaller species imported from around the world.

It remained for a Frenchman, Bory Latour-Marliac, to transform waterlily culture into a minor mania. Starting in the 1880s in southern France, Marliac amazed horticulturists by introducing one spectacular hybrid variety after another in a rainbow of hues. It is likely that he began hybridizing by crossing the white European

Dressed in middy blouse and sailor's hat, a stalwart British child pretends to go punting on the platter-sized lily pad of a Victoria waterlily in this illustration from the January 1885 issue of The Garden Chronicle. Said to be strong enough to support a man, the Victoria lily pad gets its buoyancy from a network of radiating veins that project skeleton-fashion from its undersurface, trapping air in a honeycomb of interlocking pockets under the lily pad's skin.

THE MARLIAC HYBRIDS

waterlily with the New England pond lily, as well as with a pink variety called the Cape Cod waterlily and with a yellow variety from Florida. No one can ever be sure, for he kept his records in his head and they died with him in 1911. The number of popular varieties that still have Marliac in their names, however, testifies to his horticultural wizardry.

His dedication was matched by that of another Frenchman, although the wizardry of Claude Monet was of an altogether different type. In the early 1880s, the Impressionist painter moved to a country house, where he planted a water garden. There he created 236 paintings of his lily pond, probably the ultimate tribute of any one artist to a single flower.

AN ABUNDANCE OF OPTIONS

Thanks to the efforts of Marliac and later hybridizers, gardeners can choose among hundreds of varieties of waterlilies plus a number of other aquatic plants. The waterlily family includes all the true waterlilies, members of the genus *Nymphaea;* the giant waterlily *Victoria regia,* more correctly known as *Victoria amazonica,* and its cousin *V. cruziana;* the genus *Nelumbo,* which includes the lotus that was the sacred flower of ancient India and China, a plant that holds its spectacular blooms and parasol-shaped leaves several feet above the water; and the genus *Nuphar,* called yellow pond lily, cow lily or spatterdock, with species that grow wild in ponds and streams of North America and other parts of the world.

While interest in aquatic gardening was developing, another significant trend was under way. The grand formal gardens inspired by the Renaissance had reached their zenith, and a new cult of "naturalism" arose in reaction, chiefly in England. As early as 1711

(continued on page 14)

Pioneering with rocks and pools

In 1911, when the rage for alpine plants was at its height in Britain, the Royal Horticultural Society decided to construct a rock garden on a 1½-acre hillside site that was part of its newly acquired property at Wisley, 20 miles southwest of London. A novelty then—there had never before been a public garden devoted to this kind of plant—Wisley was a challenge for its designer, J. L. Pulham. More than 550 tons of sandstone were carried to the site by train and tramway from a quarry 40 miles away, and 65,000 plants were gradually assembled.

Although several natural ponds already graced the property, Pulham added a series of concrete pools and waterfalls stepping down the hillside, and gave the lower pools shallow edges that overflowed from time to time to form small bogs because, he said, "a rock garden without damp and sedgy places . . . might as well be likened to Hamlet without the ghost." Wisley's plantings have changed and grown over the years, but it still is a classic example of what a rock garden should be.

A footbridge, its posts wrapped with wisteria, skims a lily pond at Wisley. Marsh marigolds brighten the boggy bank.

The grace that comes with age

White markers identify newly planted specimens in this 1914 Wisley photograph.

Though the rock garden at Wisley has acquired some new paths and plants, it still retains much of its original charm. Tall trees surround the garden just as they did when it was new in 1911, and the contours of the rocky hillside are softened by the same kinds of small trees and shrubs, many of them dwarf conifers.

On the cool and moist northern slope, ramondas are tucked into the rocky crevices, just as the garden's designer specified they should be. A weeping cherry that was a mere sapling in a 1914 photograph *(left)* has become a dense, cascading tree *(below)*, and a Japanese larch—the oldest tree in the garden—is still standing at the edge of a pool, its foliage carefully pruned into cloudlike tufts.

At the height of its spring display, Wisley's terraced southwestern slope is alive with the color of plants tucked among its rocks. The large shrub at left is a Lawson false cypress. Newer plantings include a rhododendron (lower right), purple bugleweed, and pink and white spring heath.

Water pumped to the top of the rock garden and stored in a 12,000-gallon tank camouflaged as a thatched cottage eventually works its way down to these natural lily ponds. A new flagstone path (left) winds around one of the ponds, past an evergreen barberry shrub, spiny alyssum, St.-John's-wort and heather.

ALPINE
DANDELION

LOWLAND
DANDELION

Alpine plants, when compared with the same species growing in the lowlands, show extreme adaptations to the harsh climate of the heights. The alpine dandelion, grown as a rock-garden plant in Japan, has a more developed root system but smaller, more compact leaves than the lowland dandelion and is less than half its size. Long, thick roots enable the alpine to absorb moisture beneath rocks in arid surroundings; small hairy leaves slow water loss from transpiration.

ALMOND-PUDDING SCHEME

the Earl of Shaftesbury predicted that the "mockery of princely gardens" would one day be supplanted by "rude rocks, mossy caverns, irregular unwrought grottoes, broken falls of water, and all the horrid grace of the wilderness itself." In 1772, a rockery was built at the Chelsea Physic Garden in London making use of some slabs of lava brought home from Iceland by the British naturalist Sir Joseph Banks, together with an assortment of stones left over from a remodeling of the Tower of London.

It was not until the late 19th Century, however, that gardening with rocks really became popular, and the impetus for it came from the thousands of British vacationers, lured by cheap rail travel on the Continent, who went off to spend their holidays tramping in the Alps. Marveling at the daintiness and brilliant colors of the alpine wildflowers, they took to popping specimens into empty biscuit tins and carrying them home to Kent and Sussex to plant in their cottage gardens. The transfers did not always go smoothly, but in 1870 the would-be rock gardeners were helped by one of the great English garden writers, William Robinson, who wrote a book on the subject, *Alpine Flowers for Gardens*. Perhaps a bit overenthusiastically, Robinson stated that "there is no alpine flower that ever cheered the eye that cannot be grown in our island gardens."

By the turn of the Century rock gardening had become the rage in the British Isles, so much so that it got rather out of hand. Some enthusiasts created whole mountain ranges in miniature by setting stones on edge, and one wealthy devotee at Henley-on-Thames constructed an exact scale model of the Matterhorn, complete with little goatlike chamois modeled in tin. In the hope of correcting some of these excesses, a 27-year-old rock gardener, Reginald Farrer, wrote a popular and influential book, *My Rock-Garden,* in which he used humor and hyperbole to drive home his points.

"Now we have nothing but weak lines in our gardens," Farrer scolded, "vague, wibble-wobble curves that have no meaning nor explanation; our borders meander up and down and here and there like sheep that have no shepherd, our silly lawns erupt into silly beds like pimples. All is uncertainty, formlessness—a vain, impotent striving after the so-called natural.

"The ideal rock-garden," he stated, "must have a plan. But there are three prevailing plans, none of which are good. The first is what I may call the Almond-Pudding scheme. You take a round bed; you pile it up with soil; you then choose out the spikiest pinnacles of limestone you can find, and you insert them thickly with their points in the air, until the general effect is that of a tipsy-cake stuck with almonds. In this vast petrified porcupine nothing will grow except Welsh Poppy, Ferns, and some of the uglier Sedums.

"The second style," Farrer's descriptions continued, "is that of the Dog's Grave. It marks a higher stage of horticulture, and is affected by many good growers of alpines. The pudding-shape is more or less the same in both, but the stones are laid flat. Plants will grow on this, but its scheme is so stodgy and so abhorrent to Nature that it should be discarded.

"The third style," he concluded, "is that of the Devil's Lapful. The plan is simplicity itself. You take a hundred or a thousand cartloads of bald square-faced boulders. You next drop them all about absolutely anyhow; and then you plant things among them. The chaotic hideousness of the result is something to be remembered with shudders ever after."

THE DEVIL'S LAPFUL

Farrer then described the proper way to build and plant rock gardens, guidelines that still hold good *(Chapter 2)*. In *My Rock-Garden* and subsequent volumes, he led his followers up one alp after another in pursuit of new botanical treasures. ("I regard the British craze for exercise as a superstition," confided the short, portly Farrer, "but walk I must, and walk I do.") His quest for the elusive dwarf blue-flowered cushion plant *(Eritrichium nanum)* was recounted with all the melodrama of a Victorian romantic epic: "Ah, *Eritrichium* is near! Down, beating heart! In another moment I am on my knees before the nearest tuft of blue, babbling inanities into its innumerable lovely faces. There is no colour that I know exactly like that of *Eritrichium*. It is blue—the absolute blue!"

PLANT-HUNTING HAZARDS

In 1914 Farrer set out with a professional plant hunter, William Purdom, to seek new species in the forbidding mountains of China's Kansu province. On the first of two expeditions they made some notable finds, including *Rosa farreri* and *Geranium farreri*. Mounted on an evil-tempered pony named Spotted Fat and equipped with a complete set of Jane Austen's books, Farrer aroused the suspicions of Tibetan monks who jealously guarded their hills against gold hunters. After delicate negotiations with the chief lama, Farrer congratulated himself on his success, unaware that at that very moment the lama "was busily issuing a proclamation that we were all to be murdered in the night with as little fuss and unpleasantness as might reasonably be." The party escaped the murderous monks, then nearly collided with a mad Chinese rebel general named White Wolf, who was destroying every village in his path. Their second collecting season was relatively uneventful with one exception: the discovery of *Gentiana farreri,* a pale blue wildflower that Farrer considered worth the cost of the entire expedition.

Back in England during World War I, Farrer worked at the

CONSTRUCTION AIDS

Ministry of Information by day and at night completed a two-volume work, *The English Rock-Garden,* which organized all his knowledge of alpine plants and was the first definitive work on the subject. With the end of the War he began collecting again, this time in upper Burma. Farrer plunged through rain-shrouded passes where no plant collector had ventured before, accompanied by a servant he called The Dragon. There he fell victim to a fever that sapped his strength and reduced him to a diet of whiskey and soda. In October 1920, the man known as "the prince of alpine gardeners" died at 40 in the mountains he had made his life.

All through the 1920s rock gardening was something of a mania in both Britain and the United States, producing—despite Farrer's strictures—a certain number of Almond Puddings, Devil's Lapfuls and Dog's Graves. The movement languished during the Depression and World War II, but then it reemerged in the postwar years, newly infused with landscaping ideas from the Orient. These were chiefly based on the highly developed art of rock and water gardening practiced by the Japanese. The cool coastal shelf of the Northwest, from northern California through Oregon, Washington and British Columbia, proved especially well suited to this new kind of gardening. Indeed, so many alpine species flourished there that Seattle and Vancouver were soon vying for the title of "rock garden capital of North America."

But the Northwest is not alone as a center for this kind of garden. Today there are probably just as many rock gardens in the Northeast, where the climate is also compatible—although the choice of plant material may be somewhat different. And the American Rock Garden Society counts many active members in the sultry Potomac River valley of Virginia, in the bitter-cold Chicago area in the Midwest and in the arid climate of Nevada in the Southwest.

Part of this revived interest in rock and water gardening undoubtedly stems from the ease with which water, at least, can be introduced into the garden. The availability of such materials as plastic pipe, inexpensive submersible pumps and pool liners makes it possible for modern homeowners to build their own streams, ponds and waterfalls. But in the course of discovering the delights of alpine and aquatic plants, many amateur gardeners have learned—sometimes the hard way—that creating a setting with rocks and water is not the same as digging and planting an ordinary flower bed. A lot more planning and judgment are required if the result is not to look awkward, artificial or just plain silly. Nothing betrays lack of forethought more surely than the rock garden that simply resembles a rock pile, or the "natural" pool with a trite kidney shape surrounded by a bland necklace of small, uniform stones, or the stage-set mountain dell, complete with spouting waterfall, rising abruptly from the flat expanse of a suburban lawn.

To avoid such mistakes, you should first take stock of the natural attributes of your property—slopes, outcroppings or depressions—that lend themselves to the introduction of rocks and water. It is not a bad idea, either, to devote a Sunday to examining how nature itself arranges things in the area where you live. Take along a camera and make photographic notes on how rock strata lie in the land and align themselves in ledges, how real streams flow through the landscape, how water spills and collects in pools.

As your ideas for the garden begin to crystallize, seek out organizations and suppliers who specialize in rock and water plants and the materials needed to grow them. Local garden centers may carry a handful of the more popular rock- and bog-garden species, but for any choice you will have to go to nurseries that specialize in alpine plants and dwarf shrubs and to suppliers of waterlilies and other aquatic plants. The latter will usually stock, as well, the pool liners, pumps, pipes, heaters, lights and chemicals needed for water gardens—and even decorative fish. (Most of the larger suppliers of rock- and water-garden plants advertise in garden magazines and in the classified pages of the telephone book.)

Would-be rock gardeners might benefit from joining the American Rock Garden Society. In addition to a quarterly bulletin of articles and news on rock plants, membership gives them access to study groups and field trips conducted by local chapters. It also alerts them to the periodic sales and exchanges by members of surplus seedlings or seeds, many of which are likely to be from rare or hard-to-get plants from all over the world.

Attending one of these events is an experience in itself. Like most amateurs who have come to specialize in one aspect of horticulture, rock gardeners are a dedicated, even passionate breed, sharing an abiding fascination for what Reginald Farrer fondly referred to as "the little people of the mountains." The littler and rarer the specimen, the keener the glint in the eye. Consequently, as members congregate around the sales tables, they chat like old and best friends. But when the signal is given for the sale to start, they close in, bargain-basement style, elbows swinging and every man for himself, to snap up the choicest and most sought-after jewels. Not without reason rock gardening has been called all-consuming. "It never ceases to amaze me," says one rock gardener, "that in my own backyard I can grow botanical treasures of every description from almost every mountain range on earth."

STARTING A ROCK GARDEN

THE THRILL OF THE CHASE

A mountain view in your own backyard 2

A rock garden may take many forms. It may spread over several acres, encompassing an alpine meadow, a massive ledge and a tumbling stream, or it may occupy a single hollowed-out rock large enough to hold only a few tiny plants. A dry stone wall, made without mortar, can be a rock garden, and so can a paved patio with soil-filled crevices between the stones. Some rock gardens are islands or raised beds in conventional gardens; some are miniature landscapes in troughlike containers; and some are built around nothing more than a few exceptionally sculptural stones. Theoretically there could even be rock gardens without rocks—since what basically defines a rock garden is less the presence of rocks than the nature of the soil and the plants.

To purists those plants are alpine materials, native to cold, high altitudes above the tree line. The ultimate reward for alpine plant enthusiasts is finding a rare and beautiful specimen from the roof of the world, and coaxing it to grow—even for just a year or two—in a sea-level garden. The greater the risk, the greater the pleasure, for the likelihood of defeat makes success all the sweeter. And some of the wildlings have never survived captivity. Not even the skilled rock gardener Reginald Farrer could persuade the blue-eyed *Eritrichium nanum* to become domesticated, for instance. "There rises before me, like King Richard's ghosts on the eve of Bosworth," he wrote, "a long and expensive train of phantoms—all the *Eritrichiums* I have loved and lost, despite care and pains unutterable."

Happily, most of the difficult alpine plants have less demanding close cousins, which makes life for the beginning rock gardener much easier. Also, there are a number of familiar lowland plants that seem to fit naturally into rock gardens—dwarf shrubs, small flowering bulbs, herbs, ferns, succulents. What constitutes a proper rock-garden plant is in fact mostly a matter of common sense. Experts seem to agree that it is any plant that does not look out of place in a

A variety of rock plants, which includes primroses, alpine geraniums and a cylindrical Chinese juniper, thrive in a cool alpine greenhouse, where the temperatures and air circulation simulate natural habitats.

natural rocky setting. This generally rules out the big showy hybrids, which in any case do not take kindly to the meager soil—though certain smaller hybridized azaleas and rhododendrons fit into rock gardens as naturally as if they had been there all along.

THE ESSENTIAL ALPINES

Alpine wildflowers, however, are the backbone of a rock garden, so it is well to know something about their nature and how they behave. Anyone who goes hiking in the spring in the Colorado Rockies or the northern Cascades or above the tree line of New Hampshire's White Mountains will be amazed by the fact that any plant, let alone plants so seemingly delicate, can survive among barren rocks in a situation exposed much of the year to intense cold and gale-force winds. Yet there they are, springing from crevices and spreading intricate tapestries of color over the stony ground, color that seems all the more spectacular because the flowers are often disproportionately large in comparison to the size of the plant.

Actually, these appealing characteristics are simply adaptations for survival. By growing close to the ground, often in the lee of rocks, alpine plants avoid the full brunt of the wind and make maximum use of the sun's heat, which warms the rocks and in turn the plants near them. In winter these plants have the added protection of a thick, constant blanket of snow to insulate them from the cold. Together, these conditions compress the plants into typically tight cushions, or "buns," with streamlined shapes that deflect the wind and keep temperatures within the plants somewhat higher. The leaves themselves are often small, and rounded or needle-thin, exposing the least possible surface to the elements. On many plants the leaves have a thick waxy surface and an inner structure of water-storing cells, like those of desert plants. Or they are covered with soft woolly hairs that shield the leaf pores from the drying effects of wind and high-altitude sun.

BEAUTY FOR SURVIVAL

Just as extremes of climate stunt mountain trees into gnarled shrubs and mountain shrubs into low-growing ground covers, so these mountain wildflowers are dwarfed. But the dwarfing effect involves primarily their vegetative growth. The flowers, which appear in the spring when the weather is most benign, are close to full size but seem even larger because the plants themselves are so small. Large flowers too have survival value. In the high mountains' short growing season, which rarely lasts more than four months and frequently only two or three, reproduction must happen in a hurry. In order to survive, a plant must burst into bloom almost the moment it pushes through the snow, and put on a floral display gaudy enough to lure insects to do their work of pollination quickly.

Another equally interesting adaptation of alpine wildflowers to their harsh environment is one hikers never see. Plants that are found in close association with rocks—called saxicoline or saxatile, from the Latin word *saxum,* for rock—typically send down deep roots to anchor themselves in the gravelly, fast-draining soil, and to get at the moisture and nourishment they need. A plant only 2 or 3 inches high may have roots 2 or 3 feet long, and may even force tiny hairlike feeder roots into fissures of the rock.

Transplanted into the garden, these tough little wildflowers demand the same kind of quick drainage and cool root runs they are accustomed to in the mountains; they cannot tolerate excessive heat or excessive moisture around their stems. Nor can they adjust, after so many years of adversity, to overly rich soils. Though a few may cotton to the soft life for a while, the great majority will turn into lusterless, overfed weaklings and quickly expire. The same is true of their reaction to tropical humidity. For alpine plants the arch-enemy is long spells of sultry summer weather punctuated by thunderstorms—what rock-garden authority Lincoln Foster calls "the muggs." Unless plants have perfect drainage and access to some shade and moving air, this relentless combination of humidity and heat will quickly reduce them to a hopeless, mildewed mess. Indeed, in some parts of the country alpine plants can be grown successfully only in cool or "alpine" greenhouses *(page 18)*.

Bearing in mind these natural proclivities of alpine plants, you can begin to plan the placement of your rock garden. If your property is punctuated by a jutting rocky ledge, by all means exploit it—lawn grass will not thrive on it in any case, and dynamite is untidy and expensive. Do a little exploratory digging around the ledge to see how far it extends in case you want to expose more of it to view. Scrape out the tangle of old turf and weeds from between the crevices, and clean the rock further with a blast from the high-pressure jet of a garden hose. You may even be able to create planting pockets right in the face of the actual stone. But if you plan to do this, be sure to get rid of all the roots of existing plants—which otherwise could return to plague you. It is also a good idea to replace the existing soil in these pockets with the ideal mixture for rock plants described on page 36.

If your property does not have a ready-made stone outcropping—and few gardens do—you will have to import stones. But that gives you the option of putting your rock garden exactly where you want it. At the turn of the century, when rock gardening was young, the idea was to place these gardens where they would be encountered unexpectedly as one strolled over the grounds of a large estate; they were supposed to be "surprises of nature." It is a little difficult

DANGERS IN THE MUGGS

BRINGING THE ROCKS IN

to create surprises of this kind on a 50-by-100-foot lot, and anyway the concept of rock gardens has changed. Once they were conceived as naturalized gardens; now they are often frankly man-made affairs, incorporating such rectilinear architectural elements as stone walls, raised beds and paved walkways and steps.

Where you put a rock garden depends partly on your personal preference: you will naturally want to place it where you will most enjoy looking at it. But you will save yourself a lot of later trouble if you also weigh the needs of the plants. With a few exceptions—notably such shade plants as ferns and woodland wildflowers—rock plants need plenty of sun, half a day's worth at least. This rules out the proximity of trees, which are also apt to invade rock gardens with their roots, robbing the plants of nutrients and moisture.

LIGHT WITHOUT HEAT

Though they require sun, most alpine plants need to be protected from baking heat. In a few parts of the country where summers are truly cool, such as the Pacific Northwest, a rock garden can face in almost any direction. But elsewhere, even in the Northeast and North Central states, an eastern or northern exposure is advisable. If a southern or western exposure is unavoidable, the hot sun of midday and late afternoon should be filtered through the foliage of trees—but trees distant enough to avoid the problems of root invasion. And particularly sensitive plants, like saxifrages and rock jasmines, can be grown in the shade of rocks or low shrubs that are part of the garden.

Because good drainage is probably the single most important growing condition for alpine plants, a rock garden should take advantage of the land's natural contours. A slope, even a slight one, will help to move rain water downhill after it has percolated into the ground. But if the site is nearly level or the soil is heavy clay, some additional measures may be needed. One way to improve drainage is to excavate the garden 18 inches to 2 feet, and put in a layer of assorted stones, broken rocks and coarse gravel, 6 to 12 inches deep. Top this with a couple of inches of stone chips or coarse sand to prevent soil from washing down and clogging the drainage bed. Then lay down the rocks and soil that will form the garden's surface.

THE NATURAL LOOK

These surface rocks are of course the garden's very foundation, the elements that establish its essential character, and their selection and placement are critical. Today, as in Reginald Farrer's day, the most common mistake in working with them is creating a "dog's grave"—using too many rocks too small in size, and of too many different kinds. The result is a garden that looks more like a geological display than a natural feature of the landscape. But this can be avoided with a few simple guidelines. First, limit the choice of rock to a single kind, and pick a kind that is relatively neutral in coloring. Also, avoid rocks that have been too obviously finished by human hands—a rock garden is not a showcase for the quarrier's craft. And finally, if possible, choose a rock that is native to your area. Not only will it look more at home in your garden, but it will save you the expense of trucking in unusual rocks from far away.

One of the best and most widely distributed rocks for rock gardens is sandstone. It is a pleasing yet unobtrusive color, ranging from a light yellowish-gray to a dark reddish-brown, depending on where it is found. Sandstone is a strong rock but it is soft enough to weather into interesting stratified patterns, and porous enough to retain moisture—a benefit to plants growing around it during hot, dry weather. And because its chemical composition is relatively

VIRTUES OF SANDSTONE

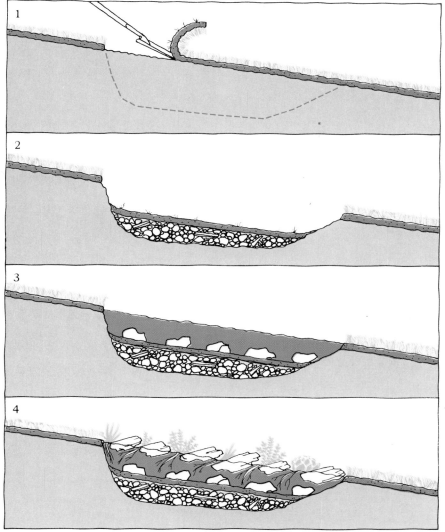

STARTING ON A SMALL SCALE

1. *To build a small, easy-to-care-for rock garden on a gentle slope, strip turf and topsoil from an area no larger than 6-by-6 feet. Then dig a hole with sloping sides that is about 18 inches deep at the center. Reserve excavated materials in separate piles for later use.*

2. *Line the hole with a 6-inch layer of coarse drainage material such as broken bricks or stones. On top place the turf upside down to keep soil from sifting into the drainage bed. Stone chips or coarse sand can be substituted for the turf.*

3. *Top the drainage layer with several good-sized rocks to support other rocks that will be exposed to view in the finished garden. Mix the excavated soil with equal parts of leaf mold and gravel, fill the hole with this mixture and rake it smooth. Wet the mixture and let it settle for a few days, filling any low spots that develop with additional mix.*

4. *Embed several large rocks in the soil mix with their broadest sides down and angled so water will drain back into the soil. Cover the rocks to at least one third of their depth with the soil mix. Set plants between the rocks.*

neutral, it will accommodate plants with a wide spectrum of soil preferences, from slightly acid to alkaline.

Another good choice is limestone, which is usually gray in color. It too weathers into interesting patterns of cracks and crevices, and is porous and water-retentive. True, a small amount of lime will leach out of it, which could be a problem for plants that need acid soils, such as heathers and azaleas. But many choice alpine plants are native to limestone mountains. If you want to make very sure that acid-loving plants are not harmed by the lime, place them at the top of the rock garden, above the lime runoff.

FROM GNEISS TO TUFA

Other rocks that are suitable for gardens are gneiss, a layered rock that usually comes in a handsome dark gray color with wavy lighter bands running through it, and both shale and schist, though certain kinds of these rocks are soft and brittle, and tend to crumble around the edges. Two porous rocks that are often commercially available are lava, a volcanic rock, and tufa, formed of limestone sediment in springs and streams. Granite, exceptionally hard and fine-grained, weathers very slowly and, being nonporous, is less hospitable to plants. However, many gardens have been built of granite when it is the only rock available. Glacial boulders, commonly of granite and abundant in certain areas like New England, are not only hard but also rounded and smooth. They are ideal for simulating a boulder-strewn alpine meadow, but are less easy to work with than craggy rocks with flat tops and many crevices.

Rock gardens look best when the rocks are few and relatively large, and are buried deep in the ground. But handling big rocks calls for some special precautions. Wear heavy gloves with leather

(continued on page 29)

A garden of concrete delights

An unconventional but imaginative rock garden near Berkeley, California, displays stones that are made by hand and plantings that take many liberties with traditional rock-garden design. The owner of the garden, a science teacher, derived his inspiration from the glacial washes of the High Sierras. "I tried," he recalls, "to recapture the power of that landscape—the contrast of dark green islands of conifers against a sea of light gray granite."

Concrete—more than 150 cubic yards of it—has been carefully shaped and textured in order to give the effect of weathered granite. It has been used to construct a 12-foot cliff on the sloping half-acre lot, in addition to 15 benches, 45 planters, 19 pools and hundreds of steppingstones. Every piece is shaped by hand, without molds, using concrete the consistency of modeling clay, with surfaces that encourage the growth of mosses and algae. Although the meandering pathways of the garden wander through a dozen separate areas, all are elements in the total design.

Concrete steps, rounded at the edges, lead through a garden of succulents, strawberries, Cape primroses, cacti and ferns.

Variations on a color scheme

Several thousand plants, from a familiar fuchsia to a rare South African calla lily, enliven this unorthodox rock garden. Many of the plant combinations appear haphazard—a prickly desert succulent is placed next to a delicate baby blue-eyes; azaleas and rosemary share a common space. Yet this seemingly discordant design has been carefully orchestrated. Dark areas of the garden, dominated by what its owner calls "Persian-carpet colors" of blue, violet, red and dark green, are played against lighter areas in which the dominant flower colors are pink, rose, yellow and white. The gray-green of foliage plants such as lamb's ear, snow-in-summer and Mexican snowball highlight the colors, and gray stone unifies the scene.

In a fascinating study in contrasting forms, an echeveria unfurls its rosette of fluted red-rimmed leaves amid the scarlet spires of Rochea coccinea. Behind the two succulents is a third, the swollen leaves of silver bract.

Golden arborvitae brighten a corner of the garden, providing a backdrop for pink coral-bells and, unexpectedly, a small pink rose—a plant normally considered unsuitable for rock gardens. In the foreground is the deeper pink of a strawberry.

To make the garden paths more visible at night they are punctuated at the sharpest curves with paler gray-leaved plants, including lamb's ear, golden tuft alyssum and Gazania uniflora. A coppery echeveria with frilled leaves serves as a foil.

palms and work shoes with reinforced steel toes. When lifting any rock, squat in front of it, grasp it firmly and then stand up, keeping your back straight; this will force your leg muscles rather than your back to take the brunt of the load. Skid unliftable rocks with the help of a crowbar and rollers, or a piece of plywood *(page 30)*. By such means you can probably maneuver rocks weighing 100 pounds or more into place by yourself. The key rocks in a fair-sized ledge garden, however, may weigh as much as half a ton; for them you will clearly need the help of a stone contractor or rock specialist with mechanized equipment.

To avoid unnecessary work it is a good idea to sketch out various arrangements of rocks on paper, and then plot them on the ground, using newspapers, stakes and string. When the plan seems right, begin to set the rocks in place, starting at the bottom of the slope and working upward—much as you would construct a wall. Not only is this a more natural way to work, but it makes the job simpler. To place a rock, cut a step into the slope so the rock, when resting on its broadest face, tilts slightly backward; rain water will then run into the soil. Then pack dirt around the narrow rear end of the rock so not more than two thirds of it is exposed. Besides giving rocks stability, this is the way they are most often found in nature.

Many rocks used for rock gardens have, in fact, a natural structure, which should be taken into account in their placement; as a group they are known as sedimentary rocks, built up in layers called strata, eons ago. When exposed by the movement of the earth's crust or by erosion, these layers are visible as horizontal lines running through the face of the rock. Furthermore, wherever vertical cracks occur, they too follow a distinctive pattern, running through the layers in continuous lines, from top to bottom. Seen in cross section, the rock face appears to have been composed of building blocks. This composition suggests how they should be placed in a rock garden—with all their strata lines lying in one direction, and with their vertical cracks lined up, from stone to stone.

As you place the rocks, tilt them slightly into the slope, so that their outer edges will catch the rain and carry it back into the soil to water the roots of plants. Also, it is a good idea to vary the spaces between the rocks, leaving narrow crevices for smaller plants like the sempervivums and wider spaces for shrubs and plants with spreading roots, like dwarf conifers. Remove enough soil for each rock so that at least a third of its bulk will be buried when the soil is replaced; even two thirds is not too much. As you replace the soil, pack it firmly around the rock, to anchor it; and to make sure the rock is well-bedded, stand on it and shift your weight.

STARTING AT THE BOTTOM

RAIN WATER TO THE ROOTS

Concrete slabs and steppingstones are laid out to resemble a dry riverbed. Contrast is provided by small, dark islands and pools of deep-green foliage.

If your garden is small, you can probably tend it simply by stepping from stone to stone, but for larger gardens you may want to put winding paths and even steps among the rocks. These should be unobtrusive; walkways can be as narrow as 18 inches. As surfacing, some gardeners use organic materials like shredded bark—but these can offer a haven for slugs, one of the main enemies of alpine plants. Far safer, and more natural looking too, are stone chips, gravel or crushed stone. In fact, these can often be extended into the garden proper, as mulch for the plants. Whether as pathways or as mulch, these materials should be about 3 inches deep. If you incorporate steps into the steeper parts of the path, keep them wide and shallow, with treads much broader than the risers are high. Old railroad ties and sections of timber are good for making steps, but even more

ONE-MAN ROCK MOVING

1. *One man can move a rock weighing 100 pounds or more by using a dolly made from a 3-by-4-foot piece of ¾-inch plywood laid atop lengths of 4-inch plastic drainpipe. To start, tilt the plywood toward the rock by placing a single length of pipe at the far end. Roll the rock onto the middle of the plywood. For safety, wear work gloves with leather palms and work shoes with steel-capped toes. Bend your knees as you push so the large leg muscles do the work rather than the weaker back muscles.*

2. *Roll the plywood and the rock forward onto additional lengths of pipe. Then, using the pipes as rollers, push the rock along the ground until the rear pipe is free of the plywood. Move that pipe in front of the dolly and push the rock again, maneuvering the pipes until the rock is just short of its prepared destination. Allow the plywood to tilt as you roll the stone off it and into place.*

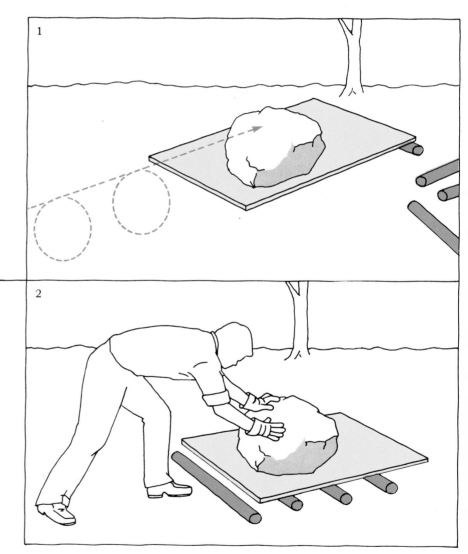

appropriate are flat pieces of the same kind of rock used in constructing the garden.

In such a setting, designed to resemble a rocky mountain meadow, alpine wildflowers are immediately at home. But a natural rock garden is not the only environment for these plants. Faced with such insuperable problems as a flat site, a soil that drains poorly, or too little space, gardeners have created ingenious substitutes. One of the most popular is the dry-wall garden and its close relative, the raised bed. Both literally rise above the problem of an excessively moist soil by getting the plants off the ground, into the air, and providing a maximum floral display near eye level in a minimum of space. "If I could have only one small rock garden," says expert Lincoln Foster, "it would be of the wall or raised bed type."

A wall garden fits advantageously into any situation where there is a change in ground level—at the point where the sloping fill around a house foundation joins the rest of the lawn, for instance, or along a bank viewed from a roadway. It is essentially the same as a masonry wall, with narrow spaces between the rocks, except that those spaces are filled with earth rather than mortar. This means, of course, that the wall is less stable, which dictates precautionary measures in its construction. For safety, it should not be more than 2 or 3 feet high, and the stones used to build it should be relatively flat. Use stones as large as you can comfortably handle, since a section of wall composed of a few large stones tends to be sturdier than one made of many small stones. As you proceed from course to course, set the rocks back slightly, so the finished wall will have a backward pitch of at least 1 inch for each foot of height; for walls at the base of a steep slope, this pitch can be as much as 2 inches.

To build the wall, first establish the position of its face by stretching a string between stakes. Excavate the slope behind this line to a depth of 6 to 12 inches below ground level, and extend the excavation into the slope at least a foot beyond where the back of the wall will be. Fill this trench to within an inch or two of the top with coarse gravel or broken rock, for drainage, and slant the top of the fill slightly into the slope; this will tip the subsequent rocks slightly into the slope too—for greater stability and to channel rain water between the rocks to the roots of the plants.

As with conventional rock gardens, the best rocks for a wall garden are sandstone and limestone. Because rocks, like bricks, can vary in color from load to load—a variation that might be disconcertingly apparent in the finished wall—you should have enough on hand to complete the job. For every 30 square feet of wall surface, you will need roughly a ton of stone. Set the largest, flattest rocks in

A CLEVERLY WEDGED LEDGE

By artfully arranging rocks that have clearly defined strata and fracture lines, like limestone or sandstone, you can create the illusion of having a rock outcropping in your garden. Using flat pieces small enough to lift easily, pile the rocks on top of one another against a slope, lining up both the horizontal (strata) and the vertical (fracture) lines as evenly as possible. Scoop soil around the stack and add plants in the crevices. Only a close inspection will reveal that the work is yours and not that of nature.

BUILDING A WALL GARDEN

a line, to form the bottom course of the wall, and fill in the spaces between them with the standard soil mix described on page 36. Add a few odd stones or rubble here and there to improve drainage, and be sure to tamp in the soil firmly around the back of the walls, filling in the excavation as you go.

PLANTING AS YOU BUILD

A dry-wall garden, unlike a conventional rock garden, is best planted in the course of construction because planting is much more difficult after the wall is completed. Therefore, as you complete each course, cover the stones with about a half inch of soil and spread the roots of the plants over it, positioning the plants so the roots begin about an inch back from the rock face. Cover the roots with another half inch of soil, and lay another course of rocks on top. Stagger the rocks so their joints do not line up with those of the course below, and fill in uneven spaces with soil or small slivers of rock called shims.

As you complete every few courses, wet down the entire wall with a fine spray of water, to settle the soil between the rocks and moisten the plant roots. When the entire wall is complete, spread an inch or two of crushed stone or gravel on the surface of the soil behind it, set in a stone or two, and plant additional flowers or shrubs along the top of the wall, extending your alpine garden back from the face of the wall to whatever depth you desire.

A raised garden can be built against an existing house wall or be entirely freestanding, and can be square or rectangular and of any size, though a bed no more than 3 feet high and 4 feet wide is easier to reach across for tending than a larger one. The construction is identical to that of a wall garden, except that the wall is built around a raised bed *(drawings, right)*. The plants in the top of the bed are, of course, at the garden's center stage, with those on the sides of the wall serving as supporting players.

ALTERNATIVES FOR ROCK

In some parts of the country where rocks are scarce, gardeners have carried the concept of man-made wall gardens one step further, and have created walls and raised beds without rocks. Sometimes the structural members are heavy, rot-resistant timbers such as lengths of 6-by-6 redwood. Weathered railroad ties are also suitable. On a gentle slope these wooden members can be set several feet apart, to create shallow terraces; on a steeper grade they can be placed close together, forming narrow planting pockets. And where the ground is level they can either be staggered or stacked log-cabin style to create a raised bed.

Another substitute for natural stone, concrete block, comes in muted colors with textured surfaces. Other building materials that have been employed as substitute rocks are upended sections of concrete culvert pipe, chimney-flue liners and the clay pipe used in septic systems. The clean modern lines of these materials lend themselves to a variety of imaginative designs, and give little indication of their original humble purposes.

For some lovers of alpine plants the man-made rock garden has taken the form of a miniature landscape, planted in a suitably rustic container. The idea originated in England, and the favorite containers were old stone watering troughs. As these antique items became increasingly difficult to find, gardeners made artificial ones out of concrete, substituting peat moss for the gravel and vermiculite or perlite for the sand usually used in making concrete. This mixture, with cement and water, gave the trough a stonelike look; it also made the container more porous and lighter in weight than it would have been otherwise.

Using the same formula, other gardeners varied the theme and made artificial rocks ranging in size from steppingstones to billiard-table-sized boulders with built-in planting pockets. The latter are hardly a do-it-yourself project, but smaller rocks are easy to cast and use. First, make a form by digging a hole in the ground, leaving the bottom somewhat irregular. Press small pieces of oiled stone into the soil here and there, to create planting pockets. Then mix the concrete, using 1 part portland cement to 1½ parts fine peat moss and 1½ parts perlite or vermiculite; you can tint this mix to dark earth tones by adding one of the cement coloring powders available at hardware or building-supply stores. Add water bit by bit, stirring the mix thoroughly, until it has the consistency of cottage cheese.

Pour the mixture gradually into the prepared hole until the hole is filled, stirring it gently with a spade from time to time to

CAST OF CONCRETE

WALLING A RAISED BED

On level ground, a raised bed 2 or 3 feet high will ensure the quick drainage needed by many rock plants. Start with a trench 6 to 12 inches deep in the desired shape (insets). Place the largest stones in the trench, tilted a bit toward the center of the bed. As each row of the mortarless wall is built, use soil like mortar, packing it into crevices. Stagger vertical joints like brickwork. Fill the bottom of the bed with ordinary garden soil. Fill the top of the bed with a 10-inch layer of equal parts garden loam, leaf mold and gravel. As you build, fill some crevices with planting mix and put plants in them. Plant the bed and mulch with 2 inches of crushed stone.

Rock gardens in miniature

In the 1930s, English rock gardeners discovered that old stone watering troughs made good and appropriately rough-hewn containers for finicky alpine plants that did not adapt readily to life in a conventional rock garden. When the supply of these period pieces was exhausted, inventive gardeners began to fashion their own from lightweight concrete. Today, rock gardeners still make similar troughs—but sometimes for a different reason: they want to introduce a note of rugged beauty into an otherwise manicured setting.

Foreshadowing a rocky slope across the lawn, a trough garden mulched with pebbles displays an assortment of small alpines.

Trailing babies'-breath cascades over the rim of a concrete trough, blending a miniature garden into its rocky surroundings.

Sedums, sempervivums and golden fleabane surround a collection of rocks and driftwood arranged in a rough raised trough.

remove air pockets. Leave the mixture to harden for several days, then pry up the concrete lump and loosen the stones embedded in it to supply planting pockets; if they do not slip out easily, tap them with a hammer. Set the lump aside to cure further for another four or five days, covering it with a piece of dampened burlap or canvas; keep the covering damp, since concrete requires moisture to cure properly. Finally, soak your artificial rock in a tub of water for several days to leach out the lime in the concrete, or allow it to sit through several rains. At the end of this treatment, clean off any remaining bits of soil and loose concrete with a stiff wire brush—and your imitation-rock planter is ready for use.

A BASIC SOIL MIXTURE

Once the basic structure of the rock garden is established, you are ready to deal with the final components—soil and plants. While alpine wildflowers grow in a variety of soils, almost all are relatively porous, fast-draining and not overly fertile. They are usually a mixture, in varying proportions, of clay or loam, humus from rotting leaves or other vegetation, and particles of mineral matter in the form of broken rock, gravel or sand. Following nature's general pattern, a standard mixture for rock gardens consists of 1 part garden loam, 1 part well-rotted leaf mold and 1 part stone chips, crushed stone or gravel.

Coarse builder's sand can be substituted for the stone or gravel, although the drainage will not be quite as good, and compost can be substituted for leaf mold, although it tends to be somewhat rich for alpine plants and may in addition contain weed seeds. You can also use peat moss instead of leaf mold, but since peat moss has almost no nutritive value it is good to enrich each bushel of soil mix with two handfuls of dried manure, two handfuls of bone meal or a cup of fertilizer high in phosphorus, such as one labeled 5-10-5. Peat moss also makes the soil more acid, which suits some plants but not others. If you want to make the soil less acid, add two handfuls of ground limestone to each bushel of mix.

TAILORED PLANTING MIXES

In a number of cases you may want to alter this basic soil mix to suit areas of the garden given over to certain kinds of plants. For rhododendrons, heaths and heathers, for instance, which grow best in acid soils, the proportions should be changed to 2 parts of loam, 5 parts of leaf mold (preferably from the leaves of oak or beech trees, which are very acid), and 1 part of coarse builder's sand. Peat moss can be substituted for all or part of the leaf mold, but if a great deal of peat moss is used the mixture should be enriched with fertilizer, as previously described.

Other plants with special soil needs are the pinks and saxifrages, which are usually found on limestone ledges and consequently do better in an alkaline soil. For such plants the proportions can vary to 1 part loam, 1 part nonacid leaf mold, 1 part gravel or sand, and 1 part limestone chips or crushed oyster shells. And there are, in addition, alpine plants with very special drainage needs. One group, which includes the drabas, rock jasmines and grassy bells, is often found in what geologists call scree, or talus, the rocky debris that accumulates at the base of ledges and cliffs. Another group, among them some grassy bells and alpine poppies, favors a moraine, the mixture of rock and earth scraped up by glaciers and left behind as the ice melts and recedes.

Both scree and moraine conditions can be simulated in a rock garden, preferably as they are found in nature—fanning out at the base of a slope. And both require, above all, first-class drainage. Excavate the area to a depth of at least 2 feet below the eventual soil level, and line the excavation with an 8-inch layer of coarse stones, broken bricks or building rubble, such as bits of concrete. Over this drainage bed place a layer of salt hay, unrotted leaves or gravel, to prevent the soil from sifting down into it. Then prepare the soil. First, blend together 1 part garden loam with 2 parts leaf mold or peat moss, adding a handful or two of dried manure or bone meal to each bushel for enrichment. Then combine this soil mix with gravel or stone chips, using 4 parts of gravel or chips to 1 part of mix.

SCREES AND MORAINES

POCKETED PLANTS IN A TOWER OF TUFA

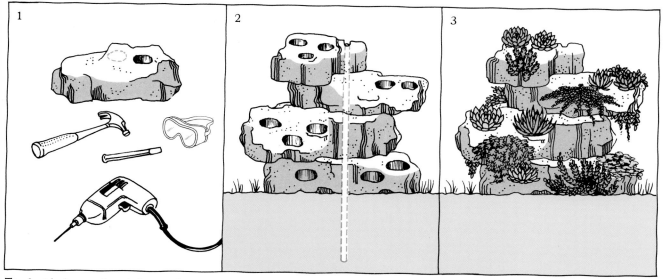

To plant in lava rock or tufa, wet the rock and make pockets 3 to 6 inches deep with an electric drill and masonry bit or with a hammer and cold chisel. Wear gloves and goggles. Knock dust from holes before planting.

To assemble several rocks to look like a natural formation, drill a hole through each and thread them on an aluminum rod long enough to drive into the ground. Or use rebar, the reinforcing rod used in masonry work.

With rocks arranged, line each plant pocket with sheet moss to prevent the porous rock from drying the pockets. Fill the pockets with plants in a mix of 1 part soil, 1 part gravel and 1 part leaf mold. Water frequently.

For a scree garden, this mixture is simply placed on top of the drainage bed, but for a moraine garden some sort of constantly moving underground water must be provided. In dry periods, it must come from your own plumbing system. In one arrangement it flows in a steady trickle during the growing season from perforated pipe buried in the drainage bed *(drawing, right)*.

POSITIONING PLANTS

By blocking out a rock garden on paper into a number of such planting areas, each with a slightly different growing condition, you can combine plant materials with as much freedom and imagination as a painter manipulating pigments. You can play colors, textures and forms against one another to create close harmonies and unexpected contrasts and, since the garden is a living painting, you can also vary its visual effects from week to week by taking into account the plants' periods of blooms. Nevertheless there are certain design guidelines that experienced rock gardeners follow. Purists among them insist that tall plants should be placed at the bottom of the slope, as they are found in nature, and that plant material should diminish in size as it moves up the slope, ending with the tiny tufts found on the mountaintop, above the timber line. This is fine when the garden is large, but on slopes of more modest size it can easily result in taller plants blocking out the view of the smaller ones. Consequently the exact reverse order may be better.

In a natural rock garden it is also advisable to avoid setting plants in too regular or geometric a pattern, which quickly destroys the desired natural effect. So too will the intermixing of too many species with different foliage and flower colors in too small a space. Instead, group together plants of a single kind, but leave enough room between groups so the plants will spread into irregular drifts of foliage—and then of massed color—when they are in bloom.

OFF-SEASON COLOR

Because most alpine plants bloom in spring and are relatively drab the rest of the year, the garden design should include some plants that vary from the norm. Look for species that bloom earlier than usual, like the drabas, or that have brilliant autumn foliage, like most alpine crane's-bills. Also, look for alpines whose leaves are as interesting as their flowers—either in texture or color; the sempervivums and ajugas are typical examples. To extend the garden's period of bloom, add some nonalpine plants to its composition. Small bulbs like snowdrops, winter aconite, dwarf iris and crocus—all of which bloom very early in spring—blend naturally into an alpine garden. So do such summer-flowering perennials as the campanulas; and for fall and winter color, there are the heaths and heathers.

After the garden is created on paper, it is time to create it outdoors. This can be done any time during the growing season, but spring or fall is preferable; the hot, muggy weather of midsummer is hard on you and also on alpine plants. Most rock gardeners like to start their gardens in spring, when plants are most available. But this means condensing a great deal of work into a relatively short span of time, since the preliminaries to planting—the actual creation of the rocky setting—can take as long as several weeks. Also these preliminaries should include a thorough soaking and a resting period of a week or more, to allow the soil to settle into place.

For this reason some gardeners find fall planting more convenient. A garden started at this season also has the added advantage of encouraging the development of strong roots, since the plants at that stage have completed their top growth and are preparing themselves for the winter. If you do decide to plant in the fall, however, plan to do so at least a month before the first heavy frost, so that the tender new roots will not be torn by heaving ground.

The actual planting should proceed from large plants to small; plant dwarf trees and shrubs first, then work down the scale to the smallest specimens. Be sure to make the holes big enough to accommodate the deep roots of most alpine plants. Loosen the roots of container-grown plants and set them into the soil at the same depth they occupied in the container. Fill in around the roots with the soil mix, packing it down to eliminate air pockets. When the hole is about two thirds full, fill the remaining third with water; then, when this has trickled through, add soil mix to ground level. Dress the top of the soil with an inch or more of gravel or crushed stone, surrounding the plant like a collar. "In dealing with a shrub," wrote the irrepressible rock gardener Reginald Farrer, "I execute a sort of

THE PLANTING TECHNIQUE

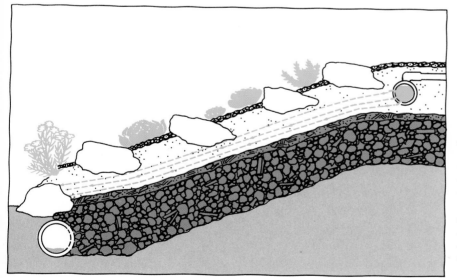

MAKING A GLACIAL MORAINE

Alpine plants native to a moraine— rocks and soil deposited by a melting glacier—need quick drainage and constant flow of water around their roots during the growing season. To simulate such an environment on a slope, dig a bed 18 to 24 inches deep and lay 6 or 8 feet of perforated plastic drainpipe. Cover pipe and bed with an 8-inch layer of stones and a layer of gravel. At the top, lay a second length of pipe, capped at one end and connected at the other to a water supply. Cover this pipe and the bed with a mix of 1 part soil and leaf mold to 4 parts gravel or stone chips. Add plants and rocks and let water trickle constantly through the moraine.

war dance round it on one foot . . . and with an alpine, I pursue the same policy on its lessened scale with a slamming fist."

In the moderately cool weather and normal rainfall of spring and fall, most rock-garden plants adjust to their surroundings with no special care. However, if the weather is unusually hot or dry, young plants may need regular watering. Make a thorough job of this, so that the water reaches down to the feeding roots and, for best results, water in the morning so the leaves and stems can dry off before nightfall. In excessively bright sun young plants may also benefit from some temporary noonday shade. You can erect a screen between the plant and the sun, using stakes and cardboard.

WATER IF LEAVES WILT

Once established, rock-garden plants have few problems. In periods of drought they may need watering—a good rule of thumb is to water only when the leaves appear wilted. In periods of high humidity they may develop mildew, which can generally be controlled with a dusting of sulfur or of a chemical fungicide. Few pests attack them, but you should keep a sharp lookout for slugs—slimy, snail-like creatures without shells. They come out of hiding at night to chew tender stems and low-lying foliage, and they can be especially troublesome in humid weather.

You can somewhat discourage slugs by keeping the garden mulched with gravel and free of dead leaves and debris, their favorite hiding places. You can also control them with baits and pesticides made just for this purpose, or with homemade remedies. Some gardeners trap slugs by leaving lettuce leaves or raw potato slices as bait, then collecting and dropping them into a can of water topped by kerosene or oil, where they drown. Others set out saucers of beer or grape juice as lures—and the slugs drown themselves.

ROOTING OUT THE WEEDS

One chore that should never be postponed in the rock garden is weeding. When weeds gain a foothold among rocks or in cushion-like plants they are very difficult to eradicate. In a newly planted garden, the surest way to deal with them is simply to pull out any seedlings that appear among the plants. Later, the distinctions are not so easy. Many rock-garden plants seed themselves, and this self-seeding should generally be encouraged, especially when the plants are short-lived, like the alpine poppy. If you have trouble spotting the difference between a weed and a cultivated plant, allow the mystery plant to come into flower; if it is a weed, pull it out immediately, before it has a chance to go to seed.

Lawn grasses that gain a foothold in rock gardens can be as great a source of trouble as weeds. To keep a lawn in its own place, edge around the rock garden or surround it with a mowing strip, and when mowing collect the clippings in a bag, in order to avoid spraying the seed heads among your rock-garden plants.

Finally, like all perennials, those that grow in rock gardens benefit from extra attention in spring and fall, as they begin and end the growing season. In late fall, after the last blooms have faded and the leaves have dropped from the trees, give the garden a thorough cleanup. Then, if you live in a region where long periods of cold are not necessarily accompanied by snow, mulch the garden with a 6-inch layer of a light, nonmatting material such as salt-marsh hay or pine boughs. The purpose of this mulch is not to provide warmth, but to keep the ground from alternately freezing and thawing, thus pushing the plants out of the ground. Apply it soon after the ground is frozen, and remove it in the spring before growth starts.

Also, in the spring, another cleanup may be in order, to remove the debris of winter storms and to repair patches of soil eroded by heavy rain or melting snow. You may in addition need to reset plants disturbed by frost. And most rock gardens are improved by fertilizing annually in the spring. An excellent mixture for this purpose is equal parts of leaf mold and gravel or coarse builder's sand, plus a handful or two of dried manure or bone meal for each bushel. Spread a half-inch layer of this mixture over the surface of the soil. Your rock garden is now ready to reward you through another season with its constantly changing display of color.

A SPRING BOOSTER

POSITIONING PLANTS TO THEIR BEST ADVANTAGE

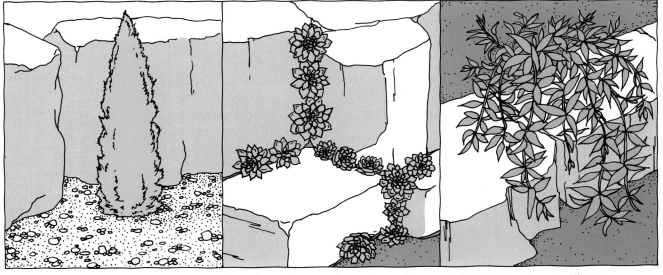

A slender dwarf conifer must be sensitively positioned in order to best display its delicate beauty in a rugged rock garden. Plant it where it will be entirely silhouetted against a large, dark rock or rock outcropping.

Succulents that grow in rosettes and spread by runners, like sempervivums, thrive in rock crevices. Here the drainage of rain water is swift and the rocks hold the rot-prone plant crowns safely above the damp soil.

Rock plants that have trailing stems, like prostrate campanulas and aubrietias, should be planted at the top of a rocky ledge or retaining wall. From there they will cascade down and produce a lavish display of flowers.

Creating drama with rocky designs

For centuries, rocks and the plants that thrive among them have fascinated gardeners. The Chinese designed rock gardens more than 2,000 years ago. When discovered by Europeans in the 17th and 18th Centuries, these gardens had a great influence on the "naturalism" garden movement then sweeping parts of Europe.

"The sides of the canals, or lesser streams, are not faced (as they are with us) with smooth stone and in a straight line," wrote Father Attiret, a French missionary, in 1743, "but look rude and rustic, with different pieces of rock, some of which jut out, and others recede inward; and are placed with so much art, that you would take it to be the work of nature. The banks are sprinkled with flowers, which rise up even through the hollows in the rock work, as if they had been produced there naturally. They have a great variety of them, for every season of the year."

More than two centuries later, most rock gardens are still designed to imitate nature's informality. Plants appear singly or in groups—not in formal rows. Paths are laid out to wander casually through the garden and are covered with such natural materials as pine needles, shredded bark or stone chips. Stepping stones are blended into the garden with creeping thyme or other ground-hugging plants. Even more formal wall gardens *(pages 44-45)* are draped with trailing plants to soften their man-made appearance.

With proper planning, a rock garden can be built almost anywhere—squeezed, for instance, into a narrow, restricted area between a path and a fence *(opposite)* or spread over a rambling woodland outcropping *(page 48)*. Such gardens can be practical as well as beautiful. The addition of rocks and rock plants to a steep bank can help stop erosion. A barren field of boulders can become a colorful alpine meadow. A ledge garden, consisting of a few flat rocks and low-growing plants, can add interest and color to a large, sweeping lawn. And a raised rocky bed can make an excellent foundation planting around a house, for rock plants are generally small and unlikely to outgrow their allotted space.

Dwarf azaleas, cyclamens, ferns and a paperbark tree, planted among moss-covered tufa rocks, create a charming rock garden between a steppingstone path and a fence.

When gardeners set the scene

A rock garden totally man-made—whether a wall garden or a simulated stone outcropping—should draw its inspiration from nature. For an outcropping, irregularly shaped rocks are preferable to small, spherical ones, which often do not look natural. Quarried rocks, with raw, unweathered surfaces, should be confined to wall gardens, bridges, steps, paths or similar structures. A rock garden should exhibit all the elements of any good garden design: unity, balance, accents, a variety of color and texture. Avoid using too much stone, for a rock garden is not a collection of rocks, but rather a collection of the unusual plants that will grow among them.

Lined at top and bottom with retaining walls built out of quarried stone, a steep, gravelly slope is transformed into a colorful rock garden. Moss phlox carpets the lower edge of the garden with vivid spring flowers.

Most of the plants in this terraced California rock garden were chosen for their ability to withstand drought as well as for their beauty. The lower wall displays succulents while the upper wall hides behind blue-gray rosemary.

Evergreens, including a weeping hemlock (right), nestle among granite rocks that were transported from a nearby creek.

A variety of conifers contribute a vertical note to a rock garden that is dominated by low-growing alpines and succulents.

When nature takes the lead

A natural outcropping or rocky slope can be transformed from an eyesore into an eye-catching display of dazzling rock plants—often with only minor modifications. A few rocks may have to be removed or added to provide better planting pockets, or native soil may have to be replaced with prepared soil more suitable to rock plants (*page 36*); but, in general, gardeners with rocky sites need only start stocking them with their favorite plants. Aggressive plants, like rock cress and carpet bugle, can be kept in check set between large rocks. Trailing plants, like moss phlox, can cascade over elevated surfaces. Small alpines grow best if planted alone in small crevices.

A variety of predominantly
evergreen plants, including a Sargent's
weeping hemlock, are planted
among moss-covered granite boulders
to create a year-round rock garden
rich in contrasting textures.

A breathtaking array of spring-
blooming rock plants, including forget-
me-nots, primroses, candytufts
and columbines, rise from a natural
granite outcropping. In summer,
ferns and heathers prevail.

A natural mound, planted with heather, thyme and pearlwort, leads the eye gently to a stunning view of Washington's Mount Rainier. Shaded areas under a stand of quaking aspen trees are mulched with gravel.

Water, the crowning touch 3

There is no rock garden—or any other kind of garden, for that matter—that cannot be made more delightful by the introduction of water. This addition can be as simple as a wall spigot dripping musically into a trough banked with pots of bright geraniums, as scenic as a series of waterfalls cascading into a woodland pond, or as exotic as a display of tropical waterlilies blooming on the glassy surface of a formal pool. Add water, by almost any means, and the garden becomes suddenly more alive.

The key word, however, is "almost." Some enthusiasts become so preoccupied with concrete, pumps and other mechanical aspects that they fail to capitalize on the qualities that give water its appeal. The most obvious—yet often overlooked—is the way water can act like a mirror, reflecting not only sky and clouds but also upside-down images of nearer objects like flowers and tree branches. A garden pool will be largely wasted if it is tucked away where its reflections cannot be enjoyed—or if those reflections emphasize an unsightly utility pole instead of a lovely yellow flag iris.

Elements in the background of a garden pool or pond—rocks, flowers, shrubs, trees, perhaps even a piece of sculpture—are as important as the pool itself and should be considered carefully before a shovelful of earth is turned. Moreover, the location of the pool should be close enough to a major viewing point like a terrace so that the angle of view permits the water surface and its reflections to provide a constant source of pleasure.

If you plan on having waterlilies or other sun-loving plants in or around the water, make sure the site gets ample light. Hardy waterlilies (Chapter 4) require at least four hours of direct sunlight a day and tropical varieties need at least five or six; with more sunlight, both will grow more robustly and bloom more profusely. So avoid placing a lily pool close to trees or buildings that will block the sun for too much of the day. If you want to have fish in your pool,

Waterlilies and cow lilies (left center) float on the glassy top of a man-made pool, lined and edged with rocks collected from a nearby mountain. A variety of ferns and evergreens flourish on the pool's moist banks.

check the location of nearby deciduous trees. They drop leaves and other debris; when enough such refuse reaches the bottom of a pool and rots, it may release gases that can harm fish, especially under winter ice. Trees and other plantings will not be a problem if they are located north of the water and far enough away so they do not create a litter problem. Indeed, an evergreen hedge or a garden wall will shelter a pool against north winds early in the season, allowing the water to warm up sooner in spring.

POSITIONING THE POOL   When you plan a garden pool, try out its location, size and shape by outlining the space with a length of rope or garden hose laid out on the ground. In the case of a more formal rectangular pool, use stakes and string. Leave the outline in place long enough to determine how many hours of sunlight would fall on the pool, how well the size and shape work with the rest of the garden and its traffic patterns, and whether the pool and its background will present a pleasing picture from a main viewing point. With a little experimenting you may find an ideal solution by altering configurations slightly or pruning back a few tree branches.

For maximum enjoyment, consider the depth and bottom treatment of your pool as carefully as its top. A miniature pool designed primarily to capture reflections or to serve as a catch basin for a fountain need be only a few inches deep. For garden pools up to

REFLECTIONS ON A REFLECTING POOL

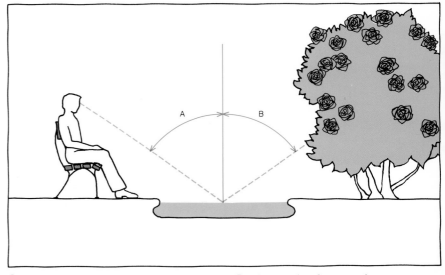

Just where you should position an object that you want to see reflected in a garden pool can be estimated with reasonable accuracy. Exactly equal angles are formed with an imaginary perpendicular line by any reflection coming from a point on a mirroring surface ("A" above) and any image-bearing light rays that strike that point ("B"). Therefore, a bush planted as shown above would be reflected to the man's eyes.

about 100 square feet in surface area, a depth of 16 to 18 inches looks better and will accommodate waterlilies and fish. A larger pool or pond can be 2 or 3 feet deep, but anything deeper is likely to create a hazard for children. Ordinances often require that pools over a certain depth be fenced and posted with "Keep Out" notices.

Since garden pools are generally shallow, the treatment of the bottom is important if the water is to yield a mirror effect. A white or sky-blue finish causes the water to sparkle in the sun, but reflects so much light that it all but eliminates surface reflections. Therefore, make the bottom neutral or dark by using natural stones, a dark plastic liner or concrete that is colored gray or black. Then images of clouds and flowers will be sharper and the shallow water will give the impression of being mysteriously deep. As a practical matter, the inevitable stains, algae and accumulations of silt on the bottom will be less visible against the dark background, and the water will tend to warm up faster in the spring and hold its warmth well into the fall.

Another basic quality of water is its ability, when in motion, to produce a range of dramatic effects. There are few sights more beautiful than the sun striking a mountain lake just as a morning breeze riffles the surface and turns its reflection into pinpoints of sparkling light. Even a modest garden pool, located with an eye to sun angles, can capture some of the same fleeting beauty on a miniature scale. Running water—a waterfall, stream or fountain— also refracts sunlight in endless patterns and adds a bonus of sound to absorb attention and conceal less pleasant background noises. On a hot day, waterfalls and fountains have another soothing effect: evaporation may actually lower nearby air temperature a few degrees—and the psychological cooling may seem even greater.

Finally, water in the garden can create an environment that will provide further dividends in the form of water-loving plants and animal life. Even a shallow water dish on a garden wall will attract birds to drink, splash and preen. A larger, in-ground pool will soon attract its own colony of residents as frogs move in, dragonflies dart above the surface and turtles probe the depths and climb out to sun themselves on rocks. If you are really fortunate you may be treated to the early-morning sight of a mask-faced raccoon dabbling busily at the water's edge. With encouragement, a whole array of water-loving plants from Japanese iris to pickerel weed will flourish in the pool or in moist pockets of soil around the rim.

How you use water in your garden, of course, will depend not only on the effects you want but also on budget and terrain. If you are fortunate enough to have a small stream crossing your property, all you may need to do is to prune away scraggly undergrowth,

TO SIMULATE MORE DEPTH

NEW FLORA AND FAUNA

WATERFALL CHAMBER MUSIC

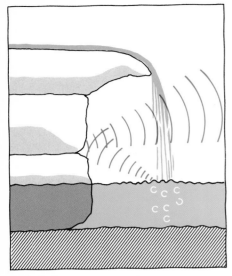

Although you can never turn a waterfall into a cello or guitar, you can borrow the sound-chamber concept of those instruments to enhance a waterfall's musical murmurs and babbles. Experiment with the amount of rock overhang that lets the water fall free at the top, the height of the fall, and the slant of the rocks behind the fall. The best combination will create reverberations and send out a pleasant musical echo.

SMALL IN-GROUND POOLS

rearrange a few boulders to create a sparkling riffle and plant some wildflowers and ferns. You may also want to build a small dam to form a reflecting pool and waterfall, but first check local ordinances regarding stream-bed alterations and flood control. And if the stream is bordered by a low, swampy spot, you may have the makings of an attractive bog garden in what formerly was an eyesore.

Lacking a natural water course, you have an even wider choice of possibilities for incorporating water into the landscape. Water gardens, like rock gardens, offer an almost unlimited range of sizes, shapes and treatments, but they generally fit one of two broad categories: either they are informal and naturalistic or formal and frankly man-made. In the naturalistic type the gardener attempts, with a little sleight of hand and artful concealment of mechanics, to create an illusion that nature has done the job. This is not as easy as it might seem, particularly if the garden is small and the gardener has limited landscaping experience. Many "natural" pools do not look natural at all. It may be simpler to stylize nature rather than simulate it, with no pretenses at all.

To have water in your garden, you need only two things: water and a container to hold it. Surprisingly attractive small gardens can be made with a modest volume of water held in some inexpensive object salvaged from the attic or basement: an old stone urn or a wooden washtub, a large plastic dish, the lens from a "bubble" skylight, a shallow metal bowl from an old outdoor grill or the cut-off end of a discarded boiler tank. Among the more widely available containers, stocked by many garden centers, is a wooden-staved tub made by sawing an old whiskey, wine or vinegar barrel in half. If the fumes of the barrel's former contents have not dissipated, let it weather in the sun and rain for a few months. Then scrape the inside clean and fill it with an initial tubful of water to swell the wood and tighten the seams. On a corner of a terrace, a half-barrel can become a bubbler fountain with the addition of a miniature submersible pump, or a pocket-sized water garden with the addition of a pygmy waterlily or some water poppies.

Such a tub pool—or one made from an old galvanized utility tub, cast-iron sink, even a bathtub—can also be set into the ground and made an integral part of the garden design. Unattractive edges and bottoms can be camouflaged with paint, plants and rocks. If you plan to put fish in the pool, use rubber-based paint or epoxy enamel—as lead-based paints will poison them. Also, for the same reason, do not use a copper container or copper plumbing.

For a larger in-ground pool, there are several kinds of containers, including preformed shells, pool liners of flexible plastic and the traditional poured concrete. Preformed shells are made of durable plastic reinforced with glass-fiber mesh. They come in circular, rectangular and free-form shapes, in sizes from 2 feet in diameter up to 12 feet or more on a side. Those that are dark gray or black give the best surface reflection and a greater illusion of depth, as well as fitting less obtrusively into the garden scene. Such pools are easy to install in a matter of hours; moreover, they are virtually indestructible, even in regions of severe frost.

To assure good results, excavate a hole 6 inches or so wider and deeper than the pool shell all around. Remove any projecting rocks and tamp the earth smooth, then line the bottom of the excavation with a 3-inch layer of sand. This will make it easier to level the pool and will help to drain ground water away in winter. Place the shell in the hole and pour a bucketful of water into it; using the water as a level, adjust the shell evenly on the sand base. Then fill the pool with water from a garden hose, at the same time filling the gap around the sides with well-packed soil to equalize the weight and pressure of the water building up inside. Plastic shells are generally sold without drains or overflow pipes. Use a hose to replenish water lost by evaporation, keeping the level a couple of inches below the

INSTALLING A SHELL

Water dripping into a hand-hewn oak trough captures rippled reflections of a Wisconsin garden, then spills over the edges to moisten the soil for primroses growing in the crevices of a limestone ledge below.

rim to allow for a heavy rain. When the pool needs cleaning, you can either siphon or pump the water out.

Less expensive than a plastic shell, and almost as easy to install, is one made with a flexible pool liner, plastic sheeting that you can buy in almost any size and then trim with scissors to create a pool the shape you want. The first pool liners on the market were made from sheets of polyethylene plastic, which tended to become brittle, tear and spring pinhole leaks. Today, polyethylene has been largely supplanted for pool use by tougher compounds like butyl rubber or polyvinyl chloride, called PVC. A PVC liner, woven with nylon for strength, is elastic enough to conform to uneven pool bottoms and to stretch rather than split under the pressure of ice or frost. If it is accidentally punctured, it can be repaired with a patching kit. One kind of liner is blue on one side and a neutral gray on the other, giving gardeners a color choice; another is opaque black.

FITTING A PLASTIC LINER

To make a pool with a PVC liner, buy one big enough to fit the pool's surface dimensions plus at least twice its maximum depth. (A 7-by-16-foot pool 1½ feet deep, for example, requires a liner 7 plus 1½ plus 1½ feet on one side, and 16 plus 1½ plus 1½ feet on the other, or a total of 10 by 19 feet.) Mark the pool's outline and excavate to a uniform depth. Small pools of simple geometric shapes like rectangles or circles generally look best—and will have more usable pool space for plants—if the sides are vertical. For large pools and those of irregular form, a bowl-shaped depression with sloping sides is satisfactory and suggests the look of a natural pond. Make sure the pool's rim is at the same level all the way around so that when it is filled, high parts of the liner will not show. Remove any rocks, sticks or roots that could snag the plastic, then line the bottom with an inch of sand. Spread the liner smooth and taut across the top of the hole—the plastic becomes more flexible and stretchable as it is warmed by the sun—and use smooth stones, bricks or other small weights to hold the edges in place.

THE FINISHING TOUCHES

Start filling the liner at its center with water from a garden hose; the weight of the water will slowly stretch the plastic down, molding it to the contours of the excavation. You may have to fold and smooth the liner into any sharp corners as the filling proceeds. When the pool is filled to within a couple of inches of the top, leave it for about a week; this will give the plastic and its considerable weight of water a chance to settle in the ground, and it will also permit any chlorine in the water to escape. Then trim off the excess liner, leaving a flap 6 or 8 inches wide around the edge. To finish the pool, dig a sloping slit trench and tuck the flap in it, covering the trench with plants to give the appearance of a natural pond. In a rock-garden setting, trim the edge with small boulders and marginal plants placed on a ledge about 9 inches beneath the surface. For more formal designs, edge the pool with a coping of flagstones, preformed concrete paving stones, bricks, tiles or wooden decking, all of which should extend an inch or two over the pool edge.

PVC liners can also be used to hold water in aboveground pools. For a small raised pool, build a rectangular enclosure about 18 inches high, using concrete blocks, bricks, lumber or railroad ties. In cold regions, provide masonry enclosures with a footing that goes down to the frost line or below, but elsewhere the construction materials can be set directly on the ground. Make sure the top of the enclosure is level. Line the bottom with sand and fit the liner inside, folding it into corners and draping the excess over the top. Then fill the pool, let it settle, trim off liner edges and conceal them under a coping of brick, flagstones, tile or wood.

One or more such plastic liners can also be used to waterproof the bottom of a small man-made stream bed or a series of cascade pools; just smooth the material into place, cut it to fit and conceal the edges. You can also use a plastic liner to create a bog garden for plants like Japanese iris, arum, papyrus and umbrella palm that grow where soil is constantly wet. Dig out a low area to a depth of about a foot, lay down the liner and cover it with about 6 inches of a

SPEEDING A STREAM ON ITS WAY

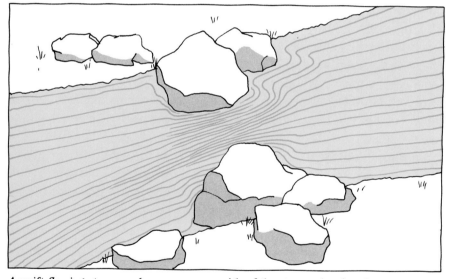

A swift-flowing stream enhances any garden. If you have a stream that is sluggish you can speed it up with a partial dam. When the water is at its lowest level, usually in midsummer, place several large rocks along each side of the stream, leaving the center of the channel open. Use smaller stones to chink crevices on the upstream side. This will concentrate the flow in the same way that partially blocking a hose creates a jet of water.

mixture of equal parts of peat moss, soil and sand. To ensure a constant water supply when it is most needed, snake out a canvas soaker hose or perforated plastic drainpipe over this layer of soil mix. Then cover with additional mix. The plastic membrane of the liner will normally retain rain water around the roots of the plants, but during dry periods the buried watering system can be connected to an outside tap to keep the bog garden soaked.

MASONRY, MADE TO LAST

Despite the relative ease and low cost of using plastic shells or pool liners, some gardeners prefer the solidity and permanence of masonry construction, which permits building a pool of any size and shape, in or out of the ground. A simple rectangular pool can be built of brick or concrete block, but mortar joints may leak unless a plastic liner is used. A more satisfactory choice for a masonry garden pool is poured concrete, the conventional material used for building swimming pools. Properly mixed and placed, concrete provides a durable, seamless container that will last for years. If the rim of an in-ground concrete pool is exposed, it can be concealed with rocks or plantings or a coping of brick or stone. (Keep any juncture between concrete and rock above the water line; their different rates of expansion can cause leaks even in well-mortared joints.) Similarly, concrete can be used with other kinds of masonry to create a formal, raised pool—a handsome feature that eliminates the problem of toddlers falling into the water and allows you to sit comfortably on the edge to tend waterlilies or feed fish. If the raw concrete of the outside walls of the pool seems unattractive, you can incorporate a cement coloring into the mix or coat the finished pool with a masonry paint. Or the concrete exterior can be veneered with brick or stone.

THE SIMPLE CONCRETE BOWL

The easiest kind of concrete pool to build is a simple bowl that does not require a wooden form and can be poured and troweled in place right on the ground. A circle 3 or 4 feet across and a foot deep at the center is adequate for a small reflecting pool; a larger size, 6 to 8 feet across and 18 inches deep, will accommodate a collection of plants and fish. Small pools and those built in generally frost-free areas can be made of a layer of wire-reinforced concrete 4 inches thick laid directly on well-compacted soil. For larger pools and those in colder areas, the excavation should first be lined with a 4-to-6-inch layer of well-tamped cinders, gravel or crushed stone; the shell should be 6 inches of reinforced concrete.

Outline the pool on the ground with rope or hose, allowing an extra 4 to 6 inches for the thickness of the concrete rim and another 4 to 6 inches for the gravel bed if one is needed. Mark the outline with a spade and start digging in from the edge, slanting the sides of the pool at an angle no steeper than 45° from vertical (an even shallower 60° is safer) so the wet concrete will hold without slipping when it is put in place. Compact the excavation into a smooth saucer shape by rolling and bouncing a heavy spare tire around inside it. Then cut and bend a piece of 6-by-6-inch wire reinforcing mesh to fit the excavation and prop it 2 or 3 inches off the bottom with small stones or pieces of brick. To control the thickness of the concrete shell as you pour it, drive temporary stakes at intervals around the bottom and sides, marking each at a point 4 or 6 inches from the ground, depending on the thickness desired for the concrete shell. Set a plank across the hole as a working platform and you are ready to start placing concrete.

A good concrete formula for a pool is 1 part portland cement, 2 parts sharp builder's sand and 3 parts gravel, with just enough water to make the mix evenly moist but stiff enough so it will not slump and run down the sides. Small batches can be mixed by hand, using a wheelbarrow and hoe, but for a pool of any size rent a portable power mixer or have the concrete delivered, ready to use, in a transit-mix truck. Pour the concrete into the hole, then use the back of a flat shovel to work it around and up so that it covers the reinforcing mesh. When you reach the marks on the stakes, remove the stakes and fill in the holes they leave. Form the top rim into a rounded edge extending an inch or two above ground level to keep surface water and silt from washing into the pool during heavy rains. You can leave the surface of the concrete as it is or, for a smoother finish, go over it lightly with a wooden mason's float. At the same time, before the concrete hardens, you can add coloring powder to darken the bottom of the pool. To keep the concrete moist while it

POURING AND SHAPING

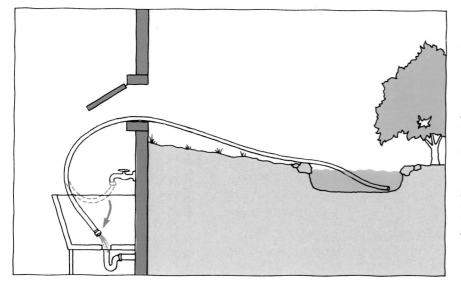

HOW TO DRAIN A POOL

A garden pool without a drain can easily be emptied for cleaning or repair by siphoning the water to any place lower than the bottom of the pool—for example, into a basement laundry sink. Place one end of a hose in the pool at its deepest point and attach the other end to the basement faucet. Run water from the faucet until it begins to flow into the pool, indicating that the hose is filled. Then, with the tap off, unscrew the connector from the faucet and insert it into the sink drain. With the hose in this position, water from the garden pool will be siphoned into the drain.

cures and hardens, spread burlap, canvas or straw over the surface and sprinkle this covering occasionally with water from the garden hose for at least a week.

Even after it has cured, fresh concrete covered with water will release lime in quantities toxic to fish and plants, so do not introduce them immediately. Paint may temporarily seal off the lime, and there is also a more effective sealing agent, a clear neutralizing glaze. Many professional pool-builders, however, rely on an older, slower but surer method: they fill the pool with water and let it stand for a week to leach out the lime, then drain and repeat the process twice more. Finally, they empty the pool and scrub it with a wire brush and an acid solution. You can do the same with chemicals sold for this purpose, or scrub with 1 part kitchen vinegar to 10 parts water. Finally, rinse the pool clean with a strong spray from a hose. The bottom can then be painted with masonry latex or epoxy paint.

To empty a small- to medium-sized pool for painting, or for periodic cleaning, you can move the water to a drain in your basement by means of a homemade siphon *(page 61)*. Alternatively, you can coil a length of garden hose under the water with both ends open until the hose is filled and the air bubbles have stopped. With one end of the hose remaining in the pool, simply cap the other end with the palm of your hand and carry it to a place in the garden lower than the bottom of the pool. Then uncap the hose and leave it while the water gradually drains away. Of course, you can pump the water out with the pool's fountain pump, if it has one, or with a utility pump fitted on a portable electric drill.

BUILT-IN DRAINAGE   To simplify pool cleanouts, many gardeners build in a drainage system. To do so, before pouring the concrete, set a brass coupling at an inconspicuous place near one side of the pool so its top is slightly below the deepest point. Into this coupling screw a 2-inch galvanized pipe long enough to reach the surface at the water level you want to maintain, and cap the pipe with a screen. Using an elbow-shaped pipe fitting, attach the bottom of the coupling to a sloping runoff pipe leading to a cellar drain or to a dry well filled with coarse gravel. The standing pipe in the pool will take care of overflow; when it is unscrewed from the coupling, the pool can be drained completely.

To replenish the water in your pool, you can also equip it with an inlet pipe attached to the house water supply The spigot can be strictly utilitarian, concealed behind a rock or shrub, or it can take the more decorative form of a drip fountain or small waterfall that you can turn on and off at will.

If you want to keep the water running, however, bear in mind that a stream of fresh tap water will make a modest garden pool too cold and may introduce too many chemicals for the health of waterlilies and other aquatic plants. A more practical solution if you want a constant waterfall or fountain, and one that is easier on water bills, is to install a recirculating pump that uses the same water over and over. It will also benefit fish and other pond life by keeping the water aerated.

THE SUBMERSIBLE PUMP

Pumps are available in many different sizes and include some that can be mounted outside the pool and others that are set in the water. A submersible pump with a capacity of 150 to 300 gallons an hour is large enough to power a small waterfall or a fountain jet several feet high. All you need do is set the pump in the bottom of the pool (propping it up on bricks if necessary to get a fountain jet at water level), lead the waterproof cable over the side to a grounded electric outlet and plug it in.

You may also want outdoor lighting to dramatize fountains, waterfalls and pools at night. The easiest and safest to install are low-voltage sealed fixtures that can be placed on the bottom of the pool or hidden behind a shrub or under a lily pad. An illuminated waterfall or fountain makes a handsome display. If waterproof lighting fixtures are placed behind the water sprays, the droplets will refract the light with even more entrancing results.

Landscape architects often counsel their clients that the simplest schemes usually turn out to be the best: a small pool with an uncomplicated shape, modestly planted, may bring more pleasure over the years than a large one with complex angles and a jungle of landscaping. Determine whether your design is to be primarily naturalistic or formal, then stick to your choice. Except for hot-spring geysers, fountains never occur in nature; their formal symmetry is best used in formal, symmetrical pools. Even there, the constant agitation of the water is not conducive to good growth and flowering in aquatic plants like waterlilies, which grow naturally in still, warm ponds. If you want both plants and moving water in the same pool, you will have to make it large enough to keep them apart.

MODESTY IN LIGHTING

Finally, if you light your garden, do it with restraint. Modern equipment makes it possible to rival the fountains of Versailles; with technical help and a substantial outlay of money, you could install an array of red, blue, green and yellow lights pointing into a display of multiple fountain patterns and even use an automatic timer so jets and colors change in a dazzling panorama of water and light. But unless you want your garden to resemble Disneyland, leave such projects to the public fairylands and limit your installation to one or two well-concealed bulbs, colored white. The water in your garden will take on quite enough magic by the light of the moon.

Reflections of the past in classic pools

For almost 3,500 years, ever since gardeners along the Nile River discovered that irrigation ditches could be beautiful as well as practical, decorative pools and fountains have played a role in garden design. Ancient Egyptian pools were rectangular or T-shaped and were stocked with fish and aquatic plants, especially waterlilies, which the Egyptians harvested for medicinal uses. Most of the pools were small, for water was scarce, although Pharaoh Amenhotep III built one a mile long and a quarter-mile wide that he used for boating and water festivals.

Centuries later, across the Arabian peninsula, the Persians carved decorative pools out of their sun-scorched soil. After Muslims conquered Persia in the Seventh Century, these pools took on a distinctly Islamic character with a particular emphasis on geometric designs. Water was drawn down to the desert from the mountains through an ingenious system of underground tunnels. The tunnels, some of them several miles long, emptied into narrow canals, which often sliced each garden into four areas of equal size. These canals usually crossed at a central pool. As the water descended from a higher level, gravity-fed jets often sent it arching into the air.

When the Muslims invaded Spain in the Eighth Century, they took their designs for water structures with them. Palatial gardens were divided into small walled patios—each bisected by a canal or with a fountain at the center.

In contrast to the ancient Egyptians and Muslims, who built pools with geometric shapes, the Japanese re-created in their gardens the asymmetric ponds and lakes of nature. Each pond, lined with pressed clay and banked with stones and small evergreens, often had an island connected to shore by an arched bridge. Soon, streams and waterfalls were added.

Modern pools are more often lined with cement or plastic than with clay or marble, but they frequently borrow from these designs of the past—designs that still soothe and refresh, whether they are rigidly formal or as asymmetric as nature herself.

A rectangular pool filled with waterlilies and water birds was an essential element of ancient Egyptian gardens, as shown in this detail of a garden about 1400 B.C.

Islam's rules for Persian pools

Persian gardens were greatly influenced by the Islamic religion. In the Koran, the Islamic holy book, Muhammad commanded that water be kept in motion. As a result, the Muslims devised ingenious schemes for moving water from one part of the garden to another, including sloping stone chutes cloaked with shallow running water. Fountains were simple, unadorned jets of water, for religious beliefs also forbade making likenesses of living things.

A chute, rippling with clear water, connects a Persian pavilion with a tranquil garden pool in this 1847 drawing. Water was circulated under the stone floors of many pavilions in order to cool them.

A wall fountain, a modern version of the ancient Persian water chute, offers a steady cascade of purling water. A pump recirculates the water through copper tubes that are concealed within the brickwork.

Spain's geometric gardens

Of the 50,000 villa gardens built in Spain during the reign of the Muslims only a handful have survived. One of the most beautiful is located at the Generalife, a 13th Century summer palace for Granada's Moorish kings (*below, left*). Perched on a mountainside, the Generalife has seven terraced gardens with interconnecting canals. Moorish designs have influenced many modern water gardens, including one that graces a New Orleans estate (*opposite*).

A small fountain at Longue Vue draws upon its Moorish heritage for its geometric design. Pebbles for the pool and surrounding courtyard were imported from Spain and set in a foundation of concrete.

Arching jets of water mimic the stone arches of a neighboring arcade in the Generalife's Court of the Canal. Beds of cypress, myrtle, oleander and roses border the canal in a pattern developed more than 600 years ago.

Inspired by a Generalife garden, the Canal Garden at New Orleans' Longue Vue estate features a narrow canal and simple jet fountains. Potted plants, including tulips and liriopes, add color to the clay-tiled bank.

Arching jets of water, identical to those used for centuries by the Moors, frame columns of a loggia, or outdoor sitting room, at Longue Vue.

Japan's homage to nature

By the Ninth Century, a lake was considered an essential element of a Japanese garden. Some lakes were large enough for boating. Most, however, were small and featured one or two islands and a path that wound around the lake to offer different viewpoints of the water. One of the most famous of these stroll gardens is the Ginkakuji garden in Kyoto *(right),* designed by Sho-ami, a 15th Century Japanese tea professor, painter and landscape architect.

A multilevel waterfall sends sheets of water cascading into a small pond in this modern Japanese garden. A simple rustic bridge—for centuries an important element of Japanese water gardens—spans the pond.

Evergreen shrubs and trees, clipped into fanciful shapes, surround the rocky shores of a Japanese-style pond in Southern California. Such clipping was introduced by Sho-ami, the creator of the Ginkakuji garden.

Designed for a Japanese shogun in 1480, the garden of the Ginkakuji, or Silver Pavilion (shown here in an 1893 etching), features a stream, lake and waterfall. Two islands adorn the center of the lake.

The bewitching beauty of water plants 4

Of the many plants that can be grown in a water garden, the true waterlilies are the most enchanting. They all belong to a single generic grouping, the *Nymphaea,* but the diversity among them is startling. There are the so-called hardies, those that will survive winter at the bottom of a frozen pond, some as far north as Alaska and Sweden. And there are the tropicals, so tender they must be replanted or replaced each year except where the climate is totally frost-free. Among these tropicals, some bloom by day and others bloom at night. There are pygmies with flowers only an inch or so in diameter and there are giants with spectacular blooms as large as a dinner plate.

Among the most fascinating are the hardy waterlilies listed in catalogues as "changeables," "autumn shades" or "sunset shades." These are one color when they open, but by the end of the first day have already begun to change to a darker hue, which continues to deepen on successive days. A large-flowered Marliac variety called Comanche, considered by many water gardeners to be the finest of the changeables, starts out a rich rose-apricot color and becomes darker and more vivid until it finally turns a glowing coppery bronze, with what one admirer has called "a heart of fire."

The hardy lilies are the native lilies of temperate zones in Europe, Asia or North America—or their hybrids. They have smooth, round leaves of moderate size—2 to 8 inches in diameter. Their flowers, which come in every color except blue, green and purple, open during the day, close at night, then reopen on a second and third day and sometimes on a fourth. The flowers generally float at water level, although under crowded conditions they may rise above the water on their stems.

Hardy lilies have large rhizomes, which are tuber-like underground stems, and will live under a foot of ice as long as the rhizomes themselves do not freeze. All hardy lilies are perennials, and be-

A placid pool 2 feet deep and bordered with bluestone slabs offers a reflective surface for fragrant Rose Arey waterlilies. Spikes of red cardinal flowers and swamp milkweed rise from the pool's boggy bank.

cause of this they are popular with gardeners who favor plants that come up year after year with a minimum of care.

The other broad category of true waterlilies includes species that come from warmer regions. Although they will not survive winters north of such places as Hawaii and the warmer parts of Florida, they are just as popular as the hardy lilies—sometimes more so—for they can be grown in many northern gardens as annuals. The tropical lilies do just about everything that hardy lilies do—but even more flamboyantly. Their leaves are larger, and are often beautifully colored and veined, with crimped, fluted or frilled edges. Their flowers come in a spectrum of colors that includes blue and purple, and are bigger and more prolific; some tropical varieties produce four or five times more flowers per season than hardy varieties. The flowers of most of them are held above the water on tall, strong stems, making them excellent for cutting.

BLOOMS BY DAY OR NIGHT   Most of the tropical waterlilies that flower in the daytime open before noon and close around dusk, and almost all of them are fragrant. The night-blooming varieties open at about the time that day-blooming lilies close, and stay open until midday. They used to be called husband lilies because they unfolded as the man of the house arrived home from work. When illuminated by the moon—or by spotlights hidden in plantings around the pool—night-blooming lilies put on a magical display for summer garden parties.

The two kinds of waterlilies, tropical and hardy, have different growing requirements. In much of the United States, hardy lilies can be planted as early as mid-April without fear of damage from frost, and can stand cool, deep water. Tropical lilies, on the other hand, must be planted six weeks later, in late spring, and need warm, shallow water to get started. Also, many of them require twice as much pool space as hardy lilies. Once started, the tropical lilies come into bloom quickly, soon catching up with their hardier cousins. And they continue to bloom late into the season, to the end of fall if the pool is sheltered from the wind.

FLOWERS IN SUCCESSION   Despite these differences, many gardeners with pools of sufficient size grow lilies of both kinds. To accommodate the tropical varieties, they prepare raised platforms and plant the tender lilies only when the water warms. By so doing, they have a continuous floral display. In spring, the earliest hardy lilies appear—*N. odorata gigantea,* a large fragrant white, for example—followed by later blooming hardy varieties in red, yellow and changeable shades, such as the garnet-red Attraction. In early summer, the first of the day-blooming tropical lilies make their debut, to be joined in mid-summer by the night-blooming varieties.

All true waterlilies, including those that flower at night, need a measure of full sun in order to produce the biggest, most abundant bloom, but some will perform reasonably well in partial shade. Comanche and Chromatella are good examples of shade-tolerant hardy lilies, and the plants named Director George T. Moore and Isabelle Pring are examples of shade-tolerant tropicals. Several lilies are smaller than normal, making them good choices for tub gardens and pools of limited size. One of the most popular hardy lilies for this purpose is, for example, Gloriosa, which has small leaves, although its bright red flowers can be 6 inches in diameter. Other small-scale hardy strains include the so-called pygmy lilies, whose white and yellow flowers are only 1 to 2 inches across.

Among the tropical lilies adapted to small pools and tub gardening is Dauben, a fragrant light-blue variety from whose leaves spring tiny miniature plants, complete with miniature blooms. These piggy-back plants, called viviparous, bear young that can be removed and repotted (page 77). Another small tropical with this attribute is Mary Margaret, whose baby-blue flowers with yellow centers are not much bigger than a quarter.

In many small pools and tub gardens these diminutive lilies are combined with other aquatic plants that are similar in scale. One of the most decorative is the tropical water poppy, which produces a profusion of small yellow flowers all summer long and resembles the land-based California poppy in appearance. The water poppy is also useful as a foil for larger lilies in larger pools. In fact, though true waterlilies will undoubtedly be the backbone of your water garden, you should not restrict yourself to them. There are many other

MINIATURE TROPICALS

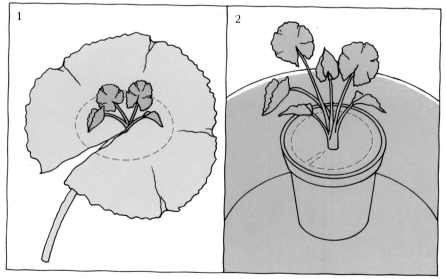

PLANTLET INTO WATERLILY

1. *A miniature offspring produced on the leaf of a viviparous ("living young") waterlily is ready to be transplanted when a plantlet sends out its roots. To remove the plantlet, snip a circle of leaf around its base an inch in diameter.*

2. *Place the plantlet and leaf fragment on moist garden soil in a 3- or 4-inch pot, pinning the leaf down with toothpicks or hairpins. Submerge the pot in a shallow tub until 1 to 2 inches of water covers the soil. When the young waterlily is well rooted, move it to a full-sized container and set it in the pool.*

useful and beautiful aquatic plants. In addition to the floating poppy, the surface of the pool could be decorated with water lettuce, which has rosettes of pale blue-green leaves and dangling, free-floating roots that permit the plant to skim around the pool's surface at the whim of the breeze. There is also the floating heart, with lily-pad leaves and yellow flowers. The water hyacinth is also a lovely floating plant, with lavender-blue flowers shaped like those of its land-based namesake, but unfortunately it has such a bad reputation for clogging waterways that it cannot be shipped across state lines; dealers may sell it only in the states where they grow it.

OXYGEN FOR THE FISH

A number of plants should be considered if you plan to put fish in your water garden. The most important of these are the submerged oxygenating plants like anarchis, cabomba, sagittaria, water milfoil, parrot's-feather and eelgrass. These underwater species help to keep the pool water in proper chemical balance by absorbing carbon dioxide produced by the fish and converting it into oxygen, which the fish need. Occasionally you can see the oxygen form tiny silver bubbles on the surface of the foliage. Besides providing oxygen, these underwater plants compete with algae for the pool's nutrients and sunlight and thus help to keep the water clear. And their attractive foliage, waving in the watery depths, supplies fish with food, a bed for their spawn and a hiding place for their young.

For shallow water near the edges of pools and the moist adjoining land, there is another group of plants that lend color to a water-garden scene. Certainly the most dramatic of them is the lotus, whose richly perfumed flowers are often 10 to 12 inches across and stand on sturdy, elegant 3- to 5-foot stems. The lotus flowers come in shades of pink, red, yellow and white, and, like those of the waterlilies, open over a period of about three days, becoming wider each day. The plant dies down in winter in northern areas, but will come up the following spring provided the water has not frozen around its roots. One popular species is the Momo Batan, an Oriental lotus that can be grown on a sunny terrace in a tub filled half with soil and half with water. It grows up to 6 feet tall and has round pale green leaves, 2 feet in diameter, and fragrant pink blossoms, 5 inches across.

COLOR AT WATER'S EDGE

Other favorites for the edge of a pool are the many varieties of water iris, whose red, white, blue, purple and yellow flowers open in late spring and early summer; the handsome arrowhead, with arrow-shaped leaves and white flower spikes; and the pickerel rush, with blue-violet blossoms and spear-shaped leaves. For early and late color there are the yellow marsh marigold, the first of the bog plants to come into bloom, and the fiery red cardinal flower, whose blossoms appear from July through September. For striking foliage there are the 6-foot-tall papyrus and the 3-foot-tall umbrella plant, both with stems topped by tufts of leaflike bracts. Other choices include such familiar water plants as dwarf bamboo, horsetail rush, bulrush, cattail and wild rice.

Whatever your choice of aquatic plants, it is imperative to plant them as soon as possible after they arrive. This means that their arrival should coincide with the air and water conditions that are best for their growth, and in fact most suppliers of aquatic plants do not ship stock until it is safe to plant outdoors in your climate zone. If you live in Zone 6, for example—a broad band that includes Hartford, Connecticut; Charleston, West Virginia; Topeka, Kansas; and Walla Walla, Washington—you will generally receive hardy waterlilies in late April. But if the winter has been unusually long or severe, the supplier may not send plants until early May. Tropical lilies, on the other hand, will normally not reach you in Zone 6 until the first week in June, when the water in the pool will have warmed up enough for these tender varieties to be transplanted with a minimum of shock. North and south of this zone, safe planting dates vary and shipping dates are altered accordingly.

Most waterlilies need a very rich soil; this is especially true of the tropicals. Swamp muck and river mud may seem ideal, but they are not necessarily good choices. They generally lack sufficient nutrients and may also produce harmful gases that turn the water sour and are toxic to fish. The same is true of soils containing leaf mold, compost, peat moss or fresh manure. The best growing medium is a good garden topsoil containing some clay as a binding agent.

CLIMATE-TIMED SHIPMENTS

LILY IN A BASKET

To plant a waterlily in a plastic laundry basket, line the container with burlap, then fill it with moistened garden loam mixed with an aquatic plant fertilizer. Place the rhizome of a hardy lily horizontally, the rootstock of a tropical lily (inset) vertically. Press the soil firmly around either, with the growing tip or crown exposed. Add an inch of coarse sand and set a stone where it will hold the rhizome in place. Submerge the container so the sand is 6 to 8 inches below the water surface, supporting it on bricks if necessary. As new leaves reach the surface, remove the bricks a layer at a time until about 10 inches of water is covering the sand.

To every 5 parts of this topsoil, add 1 part of dried cow manure (not dehydrated), or use a commercial fertilizer not toxic to fish.

If your water garden is a small pool or a tub, you can spread a 6- to 8-inch layer of soil on the bottom of the container. Cover it with a piece of burlap anchored with stones while you fill the container with water. Then remove the burlap and set in the plants so that only their growing tips are exposed. Finally, cover the soil, except for a small area around each growing tip, with about a half inch of pea-sized gravel, crushed stone or coarse builder's sand to prevent the water from being muddied.

A PLANT IN A BUN   In larger natural ponds, professional growers sometimes use the "hotdog" technique to plant aquatics. They wrap the rhizome in a thick piece of sod, grass side out, add some fertilizer, and bind it with cloth tape—something like a hotdog in a bun. Then they toss the plant into the pond, relying on the weight of the sod to carry it to the bottom, where it will take root and grow. But for amateurs, a more dependable technique is to plant the roots in individual containers, then put them in the water *(page 79)*.

Setting plants in containers rather than in a soil-bottomed pool has many advantages. In the first place, it is much easier to work at a potting bench than to wade around in cold murky water, burying rhizomes by feel. The use of containers also permits you to prepare the pool in early spring, long in advance of the plants' arrival—to clean it, refill it and allow the water to warm to the desired temperature. Containers, in addition, allow you to adjust the depth of each plant individually, by propping it up on bricks or flat stones, and to change the position of plants at will. And they make it simple

(continued on page 85)

The rewards of good breeding

In the 1800s, when the first tropical waterlilies opened their giant flowers in botanical gardens in Europe and America, people traveled for miles to see them. Special illumination was installed and newspapers reported the flowering as a major event. Yet despite the enormous interest in the plants, few people put them in their own pools. "A gardener practically needed a small lake to grow them," one expert explains, "and besides, their colors were not all that exciting."

Both objections were laid to rest in the early 20th Century by a number of dedicated hybridizers—chief among them George Pring of the Missouri Botanical Garden. Over the years he and other hybridizers introduced tropical waterlilies in an incredible array of hues, sizes and shapes. Pring used pygmy waterlilies from Africa to get lilies of a size appropriate to the average garden pool. Still, the search for the perfect lily continues unabated. No one has yet bred a hardy lily that blooms 24 hours a day.

A night-blooming tropical lily unfurls its pink petals beside day-blooming white lilies that have stayed open longer than usual.

80

A medley of tropical bloom

The only prerequisites for growing tropical waterlilies, according to one devotee, are a "hot summer and glorious sun." Those two conditions met, you can choose from an amazing variety of plants. They range in size from Missouri *(below)*, which may cover 10 square feet, to the pygmy *(opposite, below right)*, small enough for a fish bowl. Equally varied is the range of colors—from purest white through deepest red to palest blue. Foliage may vie with flowers for attention, and many varieties exude distinctive scents.

The magnificent Missouri, a Pring variety, opens its petals at dusk to display gleaming white blooms up to 14 inches across.

The day-blooming Blue Beauty unfurls petals stroked with lilac; individual pads measure a foot across.

The scented flowers of the day-blooming Panama Pacific change colors daily over their life span.

Renowned for its ruffled, purple- and chestnut-flecked foliage, Evelyn Randig also has magenta flowers.

With flowers and pads no larger than the face of a pocket watch, the pygmy is perfect for minigardens.

to fertilize plants, to propagate by division, to clean the pool, and to remove for winter storage. Finally, containers confine more vigorous species, preventing them from taking over the pool at the expense of less robust plants.

Almost any sort of wooden tub, bucket or packing crate makes a good container, provided it is sturdy. So do galvanized tubs and buckets and plastic utility tubs. Avoid copper containers, however, and any wooden ones contaminated with oily substances that could be toxic to plants or fish. If you are building your own containers, use well-seasoned or weathered wood. Also, choose white cedar or cypress rather than redwood, which exudes harmful chemicals.

The size of the container depends on the size of the mature plant. For most lilies, containers 18 to 24 inches across and 9 to 10 inches deep are ideal, but many hardy lilies will live in smaller containers, pails 9 inches deep and 11 inches in diameter. Miniature lilies can often be planted in ordinary flowerpots only 6 inches across. As a rule of thumb, a hardy lily does best in a container large enough to hold 12 quarts of soil, while a tropical lily needs a container with an 18-quart capacity.

SIZING LILY CONTAINERS

With the pool filled and warming in the sun, and with containers and soil ready and waiting, you will be able to start work as soon as the plants arrive. If that is not possible, open the packages immediately, wet down their contents and cover them with a piece of wet burlap, placing them temporarily in a shady spot. They must be kept wet at all times. For planting, fill each container with soil to within an inch or two from the top, and saturate the soil with water that it will be easier to press around the rhizomes or rootstocks. Make a depression in the surface of the soil. If you are planting hardy waterlilies, lay the plant's fleshy rhizome in the soil, positioning it so that its base is near the edge of the container and its growing tip is just above soil level. The rootstocks of tropical waterlilies should be planted virtually in the center of the tub, with the crown just above the soil level. Place a flat stone on top, to hold it in place after the container is submerged. Then cover the surface of the soil with gravel or coarse sand to keep the soil from muddying the water.

As each container is planted, lower it gently into the pool. If growth has barely started, prop up the container so that only a few inches of water cover the growing tips; otherwise, set it so that at least three leaves are floating on the surface. The other leaves, beneath the surface, will adjust to the water level as they grow. After the plant has become established, and new stems and leaves have begun to appear, gradually lower it to its optimum depth.

In the case of bog plants, this depth is generally no more than

SUBMERGING THE PLANTS

Four varieties of day-blooming tropical waterlilies coexist with five hardy waterlilies in this natural-looking rock- and reed-edged pool.

an inch or two below the surface of the water. But lotuses and tropical lilies can be covered by as much as 6 to 12 inches of water, and hardy lilies by as much as 18 inches. No plant, however, should be more than 6 inches below water level if it is growing in partial shade; otherwise its growing tips will not get enough light.

A NEED FOR OPEN SPACES

The number of plants you put in a pool is also critical. One of the commonest mistakes in water gardening is overplanting—covering the surface of the pool with so much foliage that there are no clear spaces. No more than half the surface of a pool should be covered by the leaves and flowers of plants; with a few preliminary calculations you can arrive at this ideal open area in advance.

First, estimate the size of the water surface; an 8- by 10-foot pool will, for example, have 80 square feet, giving you 40 square feet to work with. Most large tropical lilies and the more vigorous hardy lilies spread over an area of 10 to 12 square feet, while medium-sized lilies will cover 8 to 10 square feet, and the smaller lilies will occupy 4 square feet or less. So your pool will accommodate three or four wide-spreading plants, five or six medium ones, or as many as 10 miniatures.

Having filled and planted the pool, beginning water gardeners are often dismayed by a natural occurrence: almost immediately the clear water turns an unattractive green and scum forms on the surface. Millions of algae spores and other tiny organisms, thriving on sunlight and the nutrients leaching out of the planting soil, are multiplying at a merry rate. Do not be tempted to empty the pool and change the water. The pool is simply in the first stages of achieving an ecological balance that the addition of new water would only delay. As the waterlilies and other cultivated plants begin to spread, they will gradually shade the algae from the sun and compete with them for nutrients. The tadpoles, frogs and toads that take up residence in and around the pool will consume large quantities of these tiny organisms—as will any fish that you eventually may introduce.

A NATURAL CLOUDINESS

But do not expect the pool ever to be crystal clear. Although it will become less murky, it will always be slightly cloudy and green—even when it has achieved a healthy ecological balance. When that balance is about right, you will barely be able to see your hand about 12 inches beneath the surface.

If the algae offend you, you can scoop out much of the scum with a folded newspaper or a broom. Or you can prevent the build-up by installing a recirculating pump and filter. You can also use the pump to power a gentle bubbling jet that will aerate the water for fish, placing it far enough from waterlilies so they are not disturbed.

There are also several algicides on the market that are harmless to fish and plants if they are used as directed.

Fish are likely to be the finishing touch for your pool. They keep the balance of life in the pool under better control. Fish eat algae but they also consume great quantities of other small organisms, as well as insects and their larvae. They are especially effective in keeping the pool from becoming a mosquito breeding ground.

Some owners of large ponds stock them with sunfish and bass, but most water gardeners prefer more visible and decorative species, such as goldfish and koi, which have been specifically bred for ornamental use. The hardier varieties of goldfish—common goldfish, comets, fantails, shubunkins, black moors, golden orfs—will live and breed for many years in an outdoor pool 2 feet or more deep, provided the water does not freeze all the way to the bottom in winter, and provided the fish are not overcrowded or overfed.

To figure the maximum number of fish your pool can comfortably support, measure its surface area in square inches, and for every 20 square inches allow 1 linear inch of goldfish, minus the tail. Thus, a 6- by 8-foot pool, which measures 72 by 96 inches and has a surface area of 6,912 square inches, will support 57 6-inch fish. But start with considerably fewer, to allow for growth and the production of young, and vary the species so that eventually you will have fish of different sizes.

Once fish are in the pool, they practically take care of themselves. The water contains so many edibles that they need only light feeding. Some fish fanciers feed their fish only once every two or three days, and claim their fish are livelier and live longer than those fed more often. But the normal pattern is to feed them once a day with a high-protein fish food, giving them only what they can consume in five minutes. At the end of that time, remove the surplus to keep the uneaten food from decomposing and fouling the water.

One of the best things about a water garden is, in fact, the simplicity of its care. The fish are not demanding, and the plants do not require any of the weeding and watering associated with conventional gardening. Neither are they particularly afflicted by the pests and diseases that attack other sorts of plants. You will occasionally need to top off the pool with the garden hose to replace water lost through evaporation. And you will need to trim dead leaves and flowers and prune back foliage that appears to be getting too crowded. Do this close to the roots, to prevent dead stems from rotting in the water. A quick spray with the garden hose will wash off any aphids that may appear; once they hit the water, the fish will do the rest. The larvae of the delta moth—a pest nicknamed the sandwich man because it floats from plant to plant between little sections of cut-out leaf it uses for rafts—can be controlled with a safe pesticide made specifically for it.

Two kinds of care you will have to provide without fail are plant fertilizing and winter protection. Water plants, especially fast-growing tropical waterlilies, use up nutrients in their planting soil very rapidly. Fertilize them once a month during the growing season, and give them a booster fertilizing even more frequently if flower production seems to slow down, or if leaves are smaller than usual and have a yellow cast. The easiest fertilizer to use comes in the form of compressed tablets, which are simply pushed down into the soil.

WHEN WINTER COMES

In all but the mildest climates, water plants also need protection from winter cold. Hardier plants like the lotus and the hardy waterlilies can be left in the pool if the water is deep enough so ice will not form around the base of the plant, but many gardeners take the added precaution of removing any brick and stone props under the plants and lowering them to the bottom of the pool. Dead foliage should be cut off at this time, an inch or so above the root. If your pool is relatively shallow or your winters are severe, cover the pool with a piece of exterior-grade plywood or a rigid plastic panel, topped with a foot or more of hay, straw, evergreen boughs or dead leaves as insulation against the cold.

You can also, if you prefer, move hardy plants indoors for the winter. One way to do this is by moving containers into a cool place, like the garage or an unheated basement, where they should be covered with plastic sheeting, wet burlap or dampened peat moss to

CHOOSING THE YOUNGEST

1. *A waterlily's stamens change position as the flower ages. On the day the flower opens—the best day for cutting for a flower arrangement—stamens stand erect and the central disc is visible.*

2. *Over the flower's three- to five-day lifespan, stamens gradually bend inward over the disc until—on the last day of the flower's life— the center is completely covered by the innermost rows of stamens.*

88

hold the moisture in. Or they can be immersed in a tub of water, with the plants an inch or two below the surface. Another way of wintering them over indoors is to lift the rhizomes from the containers and bury them in clean, damp sand. Before burying them, wash them thoroughly and remove any old stems and roots. The rootstocks of tropical lilies can be wintered over, but most northern gardeners throw them away and start over again with new stock the following season.

If the pool is small, you may prefer to drain it in winter, netting the fish as the water level sinks and transferring them to an indoor aquarium that contains water from the pool. But simply leaving everything in place has its advantages. The weight of the water in the pool is a deterrent to frost-heaving and may spare you cracks in pool walls.

TO DRAIN OR NOT TO DRAIN

If you are going to let the water remain in the pool all winter, take certain precautions. When the water freezes, the pressure of ice within the pool can crack the walls, especially if they are vertical (in pools with sloping sides, the expanding ice simply moves up the incline). One way to absorb the pressure is to put a few logs or other compressible material into the pool. Another precautionary technique is to keep a small area of the pool open. This, in fact, is necessary if you intend to leave fish in the pool all winter; otherwise they will be deprived of oxygen. Do not attempt to provide this area of open water by breaking a hole through the ice every few days; the fish can be injured by the pounding. Instead, install a small electric pool heater made for this purpose. Float it on the surface of the water, and set the thermostat to turn the heater on at a temperature just above freezing. The heater will not raise the water temperature enough to disturb the dormant fish, but it will keep ice from forming in a circle around the heater itself.

When winter is over and spring comes again, you will need to do some housekeeping to give your pool a fresh start. As the weather warms, drain the pool, clean out accumulated debris and inspect the walls for leaks and cracks. If these are small, fill them with sealing paint, but larger breaks will need to be plugged with concrete. While such work goes on, transfer the fish to a temporary container filled with some of the same water in which they have been living.

STARTING A NEW SEASON

This is the time, too, to divide and replant hardy lilies in fresh soil, a procedure that should take place every two or three years. Wash off the rhizomes and cut them into 6- to 8-inch sections with a sharp knife, making sure that each section has at least one "eye" or growing tip. Then plant the sections in separate containers and lower them into the pool for another season of bloom.

An encyclopedia of rock, water and bog plants 5

Anyone planning a rock and water garden has a world's worth of plants to choose from. A blue gentian from the Swiss Alps, an Atlas mountain daisy from Morocco, a Himalayan primrose will all thrive in the man-made mountain meadow of a suburban rock garden. Tropical waterlilies from African and South American lagoons will bloom through the summer in sun-warmed pools of northern climates, and the ancient Egyptian papyrus that sheltered Moses will root with ease in a backyard bog.

To help you narrow your choices, the encyclopedia that follows lists 93 outstanding rock, water and bog plants, selected for their availability from local nurseries and specialty suppliers. The entries, which are divided into rock-garden varieties, beginning on the next page, and aquatic plants, beginning on page 138, are arranged in alphabetical order by the plants' Latin names; common names are cross-referenced to their Latin equivalents. Each entry contains information on physical characteristics, uses in the garden and growing requirements, including temperature zones.

For rock-garden plants the entries generally include specific preferences for soil acidity or alkalinity, since many alpine plants grow in dry soils with a high limestone content, while rock-garden plants native to moist woodlands tend to need soils rich in leaf mold and peat moss. Similarly, the entries for aquatic plants include optimum water depths and temperatures. Some waterlilies will thrive in 18 inches of water, for instance, but others like the pickerelweed need shallower water. The latter, however, survive in ponds that freeze in winter, while tropical waterlilies may be damaged if water temperature falls below 70°.

On pages 152-154, charts summarize the information in the encyclopedia for quick reference, and on pages 150-151 are frost date and climate zone maps to help you decide if a specific plant will fit the growing conditions where you live.

A sampler of rock and water plants swings in an arc around a waterlily. At the top, among bog plants, are arrowhead and water poppy, while rock plants below include an Atlas daisy and a blue gentian.

Rock-garden plants

A

AARONSBEARD ST.-JOHN'S-WORT See *Hypericum*

ACHILLEA

A. tomentosa (woolly yarrow)

Woolly yarrow thrives in a sunny rock garden and will flower even in poor, gritty soil as long as there is good drainage. The plant's downy gray-green fernlike leaves form a dense mat at ground level, and are aromatic if crushed. In summer, tiny yellow flowers appear in dense flat-topped clusters, up to 2 inches wide, atop 6- to 12-inch flower stalks. If the stems are cut down after flowering, the foliage of this sturdy perennial remains evergreen. A fast-spreading variety, *A. tomentosa* Aurea, bears a profusion of deeper yellow flowers; the slower-growing variety Moonlight produces pale yellow flowers.

HOW TO GROW. Woolly yarrow is hardy in Zones 3-9. It needs full sun and a well-drained, slightly acid soil, pH 6.0 to 7.0. Set out plants in fall or spring, spacing them 1 to 2 feet apart. Plants require little attention even during hot, dry summers and do not need to be fertilized. However, some varieties spread so rapidly that clumps may need to be divided every year or two to prevent overcrowding. Division is also the preferred method for propagating new plants; it should be done in the fall, after flowering.

AIZOON SAXIFRAGE See *Saxifraga*

AJUGA

A. pyramidalis; A. reptans (bugleweed, carpet bugle) (both called ajuga)

These two ajugas form thick mats of shiny oval leaves, 2 to 4 inches long, in either dry or moist soil and are useful perennials for planting in the crevices of rocks as well as for growing as ground covers. Both these species bear small flowers on 5- to 6-inch spikes in spring and early summer, and their leaves turn bronze in the autumn. In Zones 8-10 this bronze color remains throughout the winter, but in cold climates the leaves drop off.

A. pyramidalis, unlike other ajugas, does not produce runners and is less spreading in its growth habit. It usually grows 2 to 6 inches tall but may reach a height of up to 12 inches, and its flowers are generally blue, although rare pink and white varieties are also available. One particularly decorative variety, *A. pyramidalis* Metallica Crispa, has metallic-looking purple-brown puckered leaves.

Bugleweed grows 4 to 6 inches tall and spreads rapidly, so it is best not to plant it where it will intrude on other plants. The original species has dark green foliage and bright blue flowers, but there are many modern varieties. Some have red or white flowers; others come with reddish-purple leaves or with leaves of variegated colors—green splashed with white, or green splashed with pink and purple.

HOW TO GROW. Ajugas grow in Zones 4-10 in almost any soil, rich or sandy, and in full sun or deep shade. Those with metallic-colored foliage, however, do best when they are planted in full sun. They are relatively indifferent to soil chemistry but grow well in a neutral soil with a pH of 6.0 to 7.0. Set out plants in the garden in spring or autumn, spacing them 6 to 12 inches apart. Ajugas do not require special care, although many gardeners pinch off the flower spikes after they bloom. Propagate *A. pyramidalis* by dividing plants in spring; for additional bugleweed plants, cut off sections of runners and replant them in the spring or fall.

WOOLLY YARROW
Achillea tomentosa

BUGLEWEED
Ajuga reptans

ALLIUM

A. beesianum; A. moly (golden garlic, lily leek); *A. senescens glaucum*

These three ornamental members of the onion family are relatively small and thrive in a sunny rock garden. Their grasslike foliage grows from clumps of underground bulbs, and with the exception of golden garlic their flowers form fluffy clusters of tiny blooms at the tops of tubular stalks from late spring through summer. *A. beesianum* produces two to four flat purple-tinged leaves, up to 6 inches tall, and its 2-inch clusters of blue or purple flowers appear on stalks 15 to 18 inches tall. Golden garlic has only two straplike blue-green leaves, 12 inches tall and up to 2 inches wide. Its loose clusters of bright yellow flowers, 2 to 3 inches wide, cap stalks 12 to 18 inches tall. A dwarf species well suited to a rock garden, *A. senescens glaucum*, grows only 6 inches tall. It has twisted blue-green leaves and bears pink-violet flower clusters 2 to 3 inches wide. All three species are perennials and spread moderately slowly.

HOW TO GROW. Alliums as a group are hardy in Zones 4-10 and grow best in full sun, although the golden garlic and *A. senescens glaucum* will also tolerate partial shade. They need a rich, well-drained soil with a pH between 5.5 and 7.0. Plant bulbs in fall, setting them about 3 inches deep and 4 inches apart. Keep the soil moist during the growing season. Propagate additional plants by dividing clumps of bulbs in the spring, replanting them immediately, or by lifting and replanting small bulbs that develop around the larger ones. Additional plants may also be started from seeds collected and sown as soon as they are ripe, but it will take them two or three years to flower.

ALPENCRESS See *Hutchinsia*
ALPINE ASTER See *Aster*
ALPINE CATCHFLY See *Silene*
ALPINE ROCK COLUMBINE See *Aquilegia*

ALYSSUM

A. montanum (mountain alyssum); *A. saxatile*, also called *Aurinia saxatilis* (basket-of-gold); *A. spinosum*, also called *Ptilotrichum spinosum* (spiny alyssum)

Alyssums grow naturally on limestone cliffs and are among the most popular rock-garden plants, fitting easily into a moraine as well as between the stones of a wall. As a group, these three perennial species usually form mounds less than 10 inches tall, spreading wider than their height. They have small gray-green leaves and bear masses of delicate flowers in late spring or early summer.

Mountain alyssum is a compact plant, seldom growing more than 3 to 6 inches tall, although it can reach 10 inches; it spreads up to a foot wide and is especially attractive on a rock wall. Its rambling stems bear fragrant clusters of 2-inch yellow flowers. Basket-of-gold is a shrubbier plant with woody stems 6 to 12 inches tall and a spread of 1 to 1½ feet. Its deep yellow flowers are packed densely onto 4- to 6-inch flower spikes. Varieties in addition to the species include Citrinum, with pale yellow flowers; Compacta, with double blooms; Tom Thumb, which grows only 3 to 4 inches tall; and a variegated kind with yellow marbled foliage.

Spiny alyssum is actually a dwarf shrub. It grows 6 to 12 inches tall and equally wide or wider. Its flowers are white or pale pink, and one variety, Roseum, has dark pink flowers. When the spiny alyssum's flowers drop off, the remaining part of the flower head hardens into tiny white spines that decorate the plant through the winter. Alyssums seed themselves readily if faded flower heads are not removed.

For climate zones and frost dates, see maps, pages 150-151.

GOLDEN GARLIC
Allium moly

BASKET-OF-GOLD
Alyssum saxatile

ATLAS DAISY
Anacyclus depressus

ROCK JASMINE
Androsace sarmentosa

HOW TO GROW. Both mountain alyssum and basket-of-gold thrive in Zones 4-9; spiny alyssum is hardy in Zones 6-10. All grow best in full sun in well-drained dry gravelly soil with a pH 6.0 to 7.5. In Zones 4-8, set plants in the ground in fall or spring; in Zones 8-10 plant them at any time. Space plants about 8 to 12 inches apart. For bushier growth, pinch back stems after flowering. Alyssums do not need to be fertilized. Propagate additional plants from stem cuttings of new growth, taken in summer, or by sowing seeds in the fall or spring.

AMERICAN COLUMBINE See *Aquilegia*
AMERICAN TWINLEAF See *Jeffersonia*

ANACYCLUS

A. depressus (Atlas daisy)

Ideally suited to scree or moraine conditions, the Atlas daisy is native to the Atlas Mountains of Morocco. It forms low clumps only 2 to 3 inches high, but its fernlike gray-green leaves, up to 1½ inches long, grow on branching prostrate stems that fan out like the spokes of a wheel to cover an area 12 inches across. Its daisy-like flowers, 1 inch wide, bloom profusely in summer; their petals are dark red on the undersides and white on top, so that in bud the daisy is one color and in bloom another.

HOW TO GROW. Atlas daisies are hardy in Zones 6-10. They grow best in full sun and a well-drained dry gravelly soil with a neutral pH of 6.0 to 7.5. Set plants in the ground in spring or fall, spacing them 12 inches apart. Keep roots barely moist during the growing season. Do not overwater; if plants have too much water they may die. To prolong flowering, snip off faded blooms. Propagate from seeds sown in the fall as soon as they are ripe. It is best to start them in a seedbed, later transferring them as seedlings to pots, and then to the open garden. Additional Atlas daisies can also be propagated from stem cuttings taken during the growing season and rooted in a mixture of peat moss and sand. Mature plants cannot be moved easily.

ANDROSACE

A. carnea (pine rock jasmine); *A. sarmentosa* (both called rock jasmine)

These delicate alpine perennials, which seldom exceed 4 inches in height, flourish in a moraine or on a rocky ledge or bank. They bear clusters of tiny circular flowers, less than ¼ inch wide, from late spring to summer. Pine rock jasmine, the smaller of the two, grows only 3 inches tall and spreads 6 to 9 inches wide. Its shiny green leaves, ¾ inch long, grow in a rosette from a plump underground stem, the rhizome; its flowers are pink or white with yellow centers and grow on stems 1 to 3 inches tall. *A. sarmentosa* becomes 4 inches tall and up to 2 feet wide. Its leaves, up to 1½ inches long, are covered with silvery down when young, turning brighter green in summer, and its flower clusters are pink, capping 4-inch stems. *A. sarmentosa* spreads rapidly by means of runners to form dense mats.

HOW TO GROW. Rock jasmines are hardy in Zones 3-7. Both grow best in full sun but *A. sarmentosa* can also tolerate partial shade. They need a gravelly, well-drained, slightly acid soil with a pH of 5.5 to 7.0. Do not place them near more aggressive creeping plants like alyssums, which will crowd them out. Set out plants in spring or fall, spacing pine rock jasmine 6 inches apart and *A. sarmentosa* 6 to 12 inches apart. Keep their roots moist during the growing season, but do not allow the leaves to remain wet or they will rot. Propagate *A. carnea* by dividing large clumps. Propagate *A.*

sarmentosa in summer by cutting off and transplanting small plants that develop at the end of runners. It may also be grown from seeds, but germination is slow.

ANEMONE

A. nemorosa (European wood anemone); *A. patens,* also called *Pulsatilla patens* (spreading pasque flower); *A. pulsatilla,* also called *Pulsatilla vulgaris* (European pasque flower, windflower); *A. quinquefolia* (American wood anemone); *A. vernalis,* also called *Pulsatilla vernalis*

Among the earliest spring flowers, anemones are used in woodland rock gardens tucked between stones or massed at the top or bottom of a rocky slope. Their delicate bell-shaped flowers are actually petal-like sepals that surround the colorful seed heads; there are no true petals. Anemones have either deeply lobed or fernlike leaves. All five of these species are hardy perennials.

European wood anemone becomes 6 to 10 inches tall and normally bears single white or pink 1-inch flowers. However, there are variants: Alba has double white flowers; Allenii has lavender-blue flowers; Rosea and Rubra produce red-purple blooms; and Robinsonia has two-toned flowers, pale blue inside, yellow outside. The compound leaves die soon after the flowers fade. Both the spreading and European pasque flowers, which grow wild in open fields, bear large blooms that open when the stems have barely pushed through the soil, even before the fernlike leaves unfold. After the flowers fade, the stems grow taller, and feathery seed clusters develop, scattering seeds in the wind. All parts of these plants are coated with silky hairs that glisten in the sunlight. Spreading pasque flower usually grows from 3 to 6 inches tall but may reach 8 inches; each stem produces a single blue-violet flower 2 to 3 inches wide. European pasque flower grows 6 to 12 inches tall and bears blue to reddish-purple blooms up to 2½ inches wide. Modern varieties of this plant include Alba, with pure white flowers; Albicyanea, white flowers tinged with pale blue; and Mallenderi, dark purple. The American wood anemone, which bears a close resemblance to the European wood anemone, grows 6 to 8 inches tall, with wedge-shaped compound leaves ½ to 2 inches wide. Its solitary white flowers, up to 1 inch wide, are tinged with pink or red. *A. vernalis* grows only 2 to 6 inches tall, and has stems and fernlike evergreen leaves that are coated with soft bronze hairs. Like the pasque flowers, it blooms very early, before the new leaves unfold. It has 1- to 2-inch white flowers that turn violet as they age.

HOW TO GROW. European and American wood anemones and European pasque flower are hardy in Zones 3-8; spreading pasque flower is hardy in Zones 4-9; *A. vernalis* is hardy in Zones 3-6. European and American wood anemone do best in partial shade; the other anemones thrive in full sun or partial shade. European and American wood anemones and *A. vernalis* do best in soils that are slightly acid, with a pH of 6.0 to 7.0, while spreading and European pasque flowers grow better in neutral soils, pH 6.5 to 7.5.

Plant anemones in spring or fall, setting them 6 to 12 inches apart. Keep the soil moist while plants are in flower. Scatter a mixture of leaf mold and bone meal around European and American wood anemones after they have flowered, but do not fertilize the other species. Unless more plants are desired, cut off faded flowers to prevent seeds from developing; anemones seed themselves easily.

The easiest way to propagate anemones with long taproots—spreading and European pasque flower and *A. vernalis*—is from seed, freshly gathered and sown immediately after flowering. Start seeds in planting trays and scatter them

For climate zones and frost dates, see maps, pages 150-151.

EUROPEAN WOOD ANEMONE
Anemone nemorosa

EUROPEAN PASQUE FLOWER
Anemone pulsatilla

RUE ANEMONE
Anemonella thalictroides

FAN COLUMBINE
Aquilegia flabellata

thinly to prevent overcrowding. The following spring, transplant the seedlings to their permanent location in the rock garden. Plants that are started from seed will not flower until the third year. The other anemones listed are best propagated by dividing the roots in spring or autumn; set root sections 6 to 12 inches apart.

ANEMONE, RUE See *Anemonella*

ANEMONELLA

A. thalictroides (rue anemone)

A woodland wildflower often found growing among rocks, the rue anemone flourishes on a rocky embankment or between the paving stones of a rock garden in the shade. This dainty perennial grows only 4 to 9 inches tall and has round-lobed leaves like those of the herb for which it is named. Its small white or pink flowers, ½ inch wide, appear in spring in loose clusters on branching stems. These delicate-looking flowers usually last about two weeks. Like those of its relative the anemone, the flowers of this plant consist of bright sepals, not petals. One rare variety, Schoaf's Double Pink, has double pompon-like flowers that often bloom well into the summer; another variety, Rosea, bears flowers of a deeper reddish hue. Rue anemones grow from finger-like tubers that become dormant when the leaves die down to the ground in midsummer.

HOW TO GROW. Rue anemone grows well in Zones 3-6, but needs partial shade and a position sheltered from the wind. It does best in a rich, well-drained soil with an acid pH of 5.0 to 6.0 but can tolerate more neutral soils. Plant tubers in the late summer or early fall, setting them 1 inch deep and 4 inches apart. Cover them with a light winter mulch of leaves or salt hay. During the flowering season, keep the soil moist. To propagate, divide tuber clusters when plants are dormant, or sow seeds as soon as they are ripe. Rue anemone will seed itself if faded flowers are not cut off, but plants grown from seed take three years to flower.

AQUILEGIA

A. bertolonii (alpine rock columbine); *A. canadensis* (American columbine); *A. flabellata* (fan columbine); *A. scopulorum*

Columbines have a special affinity for rocky settings. Depending on their size, they are suitable for scree gardens, rock ledges or dry stone walls. Their finely cut gray-green or blue-green leaves make lacy mounds 4 to 10 inches tall from which, in late spring or early summer, rise flower stems of various heights—as low as 6 inches, as tall as 4 feet. Funnel-shaped flowers with long spurs dangle gracefully from these stems high above the foilage; they are followed by seed-filled capsules. Alpine rock columbine forms a mound up to 6 inches high and equally wide. It produces blue-violet flowers, 2 inches wide, on flower stems up to 12 inches tall. American columbine, a native species, has a foliage mound 6 to 8 inches tall. Its flower stems are 1 to 3 feet tall and bear red-and-yellow flowers about 2½ inches long. Fan columbine's basal mound ranges from 6 to 10 inches tall and spreads 6 to 8 inches wide. It bears 1½- to 2-inch violet-and-white flowers on flower stems up to 18 inches tall. One smaller variety of this species, Pumila, produces purple-and-yellow flowers on 12-inch stems; another, Nana Alba, has white flowers on 6- to 8-inch stems. *A. scopulorum,* a tiny alpine columbine native to the West, usually grows only 4 to 6 inches tall and wide, with 1- to 1½-inch blue-purple flowers capping 6- to 10-inch flower stems.

HOW TO GROW. Columbines grow in Zones 3-8 except along the Gulf Coast. They do best in partial shade but can tolerate some sun in cooler, drought-free areas. They thrive in moist, well-drained gravelly soil with a pH of 5.0 to 7.0. Plant columbines in early spring as soon as the soil can be worked, or in fall when plants are dormant. Space smaller alpine species 6 inches apart, larger American columbine 8 to 12 inches apart. Water thoroughly in summer, but allow soil to become almost completely dry between waterings. In Zones 3-5, protect plants in winter with a light mulch such as hay or straw. Columbines seed themselves readily and should be allowed to do so, for plants have a short life. If started from seeds in spring or summer, plants will produce flowers the following spring.

ARABIS

A. albida, also called *A. caucasica* (wall rock cress); *A. alpina* (mountain rock cress); *A. sturii*

Useful little plants for dry walls or alpine conditions, the rock cresses form compact mounds of jagged-edged leaves, covered in early spring with airy clusters of tiny flowers on 6- to 10-inch stems. In mild climates the foliage remains green all winter. Wall rock cress usually grows 6 inches high and spreads to cover an area as much as 18 inches wide. Its leaves are gray-green and downy, and its flowers are white and very fragrant. There are varieties with larger flowers or flowers of different colors, including pink and lavender; some varieties also have woollier leaves. Mountain rock cress is more compact than wall rock cress, spreading only 12 inches wide though its height is roughly the same. Its leaves are less woolly but more jagged and its flowers smaller though just as prolific. Flowers of the species are white, but this plant too comes with pink blooms or white-splashed leaves. *A. sturii,* the tiniest species of the three, seldom exceeds 4 to 6 inches in height and spreads only 12 inches wide. It bears white flowers that seem unusually large in proportion to the plant's size, and its leaves are dark green and shiny.

HOW TO GROW. The rock cresses are hardy in Zones 3-9. They grow best in a well-drained sandy or gravelly soil with a pH of 6.0 to 7.5 and normally need full sun, although in very hot, dry areas they should have partial shade. Set out plants in the early spring or fall, spacing them 10 to 12 inches apart. After flowers fade, cut back stems halfway to encourage new leaves. Propagate from stem cuttings taken immediately after flowering or by dividing plants in the fall. The rock cresses can also be started from seeds.

ARCTOSTAPHYLOS

A. uva-ursi (bearberry, kinnikinnick)

A low evergreen shrub with trailing branches, bearberry is ideally suited for planting around rocks, on walled terraces or on sloping, stony banks. It grows 6 to 12 inches tall, and spreads by taking root where branches touch the soil, forming new shoots that eventually may blanket an area up to 15 feet wide. The shiny dark green leaves are 1 inch long and in fall turn bronze-red. Clusters of tiny bell-shaped white or pink flowers, ¼ inch long, tip the branches in spring; they are followed in the fall by long-lasting red berries that remain well into winter. This hardy plant can withstand wind, severe drought, cold and polluted air.

HOW TO GROW. Bearberry grows in Zones 2-7 in full sun or partial shade. It does best in a well-drained sandy or gravelly soil with an acid pH of 4.5 to 5.5, but it can also tolerate more nearly neutral soils. Set out plants in spring or fall, spacing them 12 to 24 inches apart. Provide young plants with a permanent mulch of chunky peat moss or pine needles to maintain moisture and keep weeds down; older plants need no special attention. Bearberry is very difficult to trans-

WALL ROCK CRESS
Arabis albida

BEARBERRY
Arctostaphylos uva-ursi

For climate zones and frost dates, see maps, pages 150-151.

MOUNTAIN SANDWORT
Arenaria montana

GREEN DRAGON
Arisaema dracontium

plant, and if additional plants are wanted, it is best to buy new ones that have been container-grown, or cuttings of new growth may be rooted in a moist mixture of equal parts of sand and peat moss.

ARENARIA
A. grandiflora; A. laricifolia, also called *Minuartia laricifolia* (larchleaf sandwort); *A. montana* (mountain sandwort); *A. verna,* also called *A. caespitosa* and *Minuartia verna caespitosa* (moss sandwort) (all called sandwort)

The sandworts are mountain plants, forming low mounds or tufted mats of foliage that are often evergreen except in extreme cold. They are well suited to scree conditions or rocky ledges, and moss sandwort may be tucked between the paving stones of a terrace or walk. The plants themselves are seldom more than 2 to 4 inches high, although their flower stems may be up to 10 inches tall. In late spring and summer they bear great numbers of small five-petaled white flowers, which bloom singly or in loose clusters on slender stems. The foliage varies from species to species, sometimes resembling grass, sometimes needles, sometimes moss.

A. grandiflora forms tufts 2 to 3 inches tall and spreads on creeping stems to cover an area up to 12 inches wide. Its bright green needle-like foliage is thick and leathery, and its 1-inch flowers cap stems 6 inches tall. Larchleaf sandwort grows in clumps 2 to 4 inches tall, spreading to cover an area up to 18 inches wide on creeping stems. It has gray-green needle-like leaves and 1-inch flowers, but its flower stems are 6 to 12 inches tall. These species take root wherever their creeping stems touch the ground.

Mountain sandwort has narrow, glossy, gray-green leaves, up to 1 inch long, that form thick mats 2 to 4 inches tall and 18 inches wide. Its plentiful flowers, ½ to 1 inch wide, appear on branching stems 6 to 8 inches tall. Unlike the other creeping sandworts, its cascading stems do not root and are most effective when allowed to tumble over stony walls or large rocks. Moss sandwort creates mossy carpets 2 inches tall and up to 12 inches wide. The species has bright evergreen needle-like leaves that turn silvery in northernmost zones, but there is also a variety, Aurea, with yellow-green foliage. In bloom, the plants are dotted with tiny ⅛-inch starry flowers borne on 4-inch stems. This species spreads to form a tight carpet.

HOW TO GROW. *A. grandiflora,* larchleaf and mountain sandwort grow well in Zones 4-10; moss sandwort, an arctic species, is hardy in Zones 2-10. All grow best in full sun except in very hot areas, where they need light shade. They need a moist, well-drained sandy or gravelly soil. *A. grandiflora* and larchleaf sandworts thrive in soils with a pH of 6.0 to 7.5, while mountain and moss sandworts benefit from acid soils with a pH of 5.5 to 6.5. Plant sandworts in spring, spacing them about 6 inches apart. All of them seed themselves readily and may be propagated from seeds. Those that have creeping stems may also be propagated from stem cuttings taken in early summer, or by dividing established plants in the spring.

ARISAEMA
A. dracontium (green dragon, dragonroot); *A. sikokianum; A. triphyllum* (Jack-in-the-pulpit)

These woodland wild flowers make unusual additions to a moist, shady garden on a wooded slope. Their spring flowers consist of a finger-like spadix that is protected by a hood called a spathe. In late summer or fall, the hood usually withers and dies, revealing a clublike spike of tightly packed orange or red berries. The plants rise from turnip-like corms.

Green dragon, a plant that can become invasive if not kept under control, grows up to 3 feet tall, and has a tail-like spadix that extends several inches beyond the unarched, 2- to 4-inch green spathe. Its curious leaves are actually a single leaf that divides into three leaflets and then subdivides into five or more even smaller leaflets. *A. sikokianum* is 8 to 12 inches tall and has mottled leaves, 6 inches long, which are divided into two to five sections. Its 2-inch-long ivory-white spadix is backed by a white-lined dark purple hood, 5 to 10 inches long, that is flecked and streaked with green and white. Jack-in-the-pulpit, the most common species, grows 1 to 3 feet tall and produces two leaves, 4 to 9 inches long, that divide into three parts. Its 3-inch-long spadix, the Jack, stands under a 4- to 7-inch green or purple arched hood with purple, green or white stripes. All three of these plants are perennials, dying down to the ground in winter and reappearing in early spring.

HOW TO GROW. Green dragon is hardy in Zones 5-9; Jack-in-the-pulpit and *A. sikokianum* grow in Zones 5-8. All do best in partial shade in moist, rich, well-drained soil with an acid pH of 5.0 to 6.5. Plant corms in spring or fall, setting them at least 6 inches deep and 6 to 8 inches apart. Or start plants from seeds sown in the fall after the fleshy covering is removed, setting them under ¼ to ½ inch of soil; plants that have been started from seed will bloom the third year. If desired, transplant seedlings in the late summer or fall of the first year. Propagate additional Jack-in-the-pulpits from seeds collected in the autumn.

ARMERIA
A. juniperifolia, also called *A. caespitosa* (juniper thrift); *A. maritima* (common thrift, sea pink)

Thrifts are plants accustomed to dry, sandy soils; they take naturally to rocky ledges and stone walls. Each plant forms a dense mound of stiff evergreen leaves, which rise in multiple tufts like small pincushions from a single taproot. In late spring and summer, tiny pink, white or lilac flowers bloom in globelike clusters, ½ inch across, above the foliage. Juniper thrift has clumps that are only 2 inches tall, and its leaves are short and needle-like, only ½ inch long. The flower stalks are sturdy and very short, 2 to 6 inches tall.

Common thrift, which grows wild amid seacoast rocks, is a somewhat larger plant; its foliage clumps are 4 inches high, and its leaves are grasslike, growing up to 6 inches long. The wiry flower stalks are 6 to 12 inches in height. Common thrift comes in a number of forms: one variety, Laucheana, has deep pink flowers; Rubra has red flowers; and Variegata has leaves that turn gold in winter.

HOW TO GROW. Thrifts are hardy in Zones 4-8. They grow best in full sun and a deep, dry, gravelly soil with a pH of 6.0 to 7.5. Good drainage is essential; they cannot tolerate too much moisture. Set out plants in spring, spacing them 9 to 12 inches apart. As plants age, the centers of the clumps may rot and die out. Sometimes this can be prevented by sprinkling a gritty mixture of stone chips over the plants to refresh them. Older plants may be renewed every three years, in spring or fall, by cutting off tufted sections and rooting them in sand. Propagate them in the same way. Common thrift may also be started from fresh seeds, sown as soon as they ripen in summer. The seeds of named varieties, however, do not always breed true to the parent plants.

ARTEMISIA
A. schmidtiana (silver mound artemisia)

Silver mound artemisia is a dwarf version of a garden perennial that is noted for its finely cut silvery-gray leaves.

COMMON THRIFT
Armeria maritima

SILVER MOUND ARTEMISIA
Artemisia schmidtiana 'Silver Mound'

For climate zones and frost dates, see maps, pages 150-151.

EUROPEAN WILD GINGER
Asarum europaeum

SWEET WOODRUFF
Asperula odorata

It grows 6 to 8 inches tall and is an excellent plant for alpine rock gardens and scree conditions. The branching stems form mounds about 12 inches wide that can be left undisturbed indefinitely. In summer, when the hot sun strikes it, the foliage is aromatic. Summer is also silver mound's period of bloom, but its sprays of tiny yellowish-green flowers are inconspicuous and far less decorative than the foliage.

HOW TO GROW. Silver mound artemisia is hardy in Zones 4-9 except in Florida and along the Gulf Coast. It does best in a well-drained sandy or gravelly soil with a pH of 6.0 to 7.5 and prefers full sun but will tolerate partial shade. Set out plants in spring, spacing them 12 to 18 inches apart. They may need light watering during the growing season, but the soil around the roots should never be wet; in winter, wet soil will kill the plants. To encourage thicker foliage, cut off the flower stems before flowers open. Propagate in spring or summer from stem cuttings rooted in damp sand.

ASARUM

A. canadense (Canada wild ginger); *A. caudatum* (British Columbia wild ginger); *A. europaeum* (European wild ginger); *A. shuttleworthii,* also called *A. grandiflorum* (mottled wild ginger)

The heart-shaped leaves of the wild gingers are useful for carpeting a woodland rock garden or a shaded area under shrubs or trees on a rocky slope. These hardy perennials usually grow 6 to 12 inches tall from fleshy underground stems, the rhizomes, which have a ginger-like scent and flavor. They spread rapidly, and the foliage of all but Canada wild ginger is evergreen. In spring, small cup-shaped brown or red flowers, about 1 inch long, bloom on short stems under the foliage; sometimes they appear even before the leaves totally unfold. The flowers remain in bloom as long as four weeks, until their large seeds ripen. Canada wild ginger grows up to 12 inches tall. It has soft, hairy leaves, 2 to 7 inches wide, and a 1-inch brownish-purple flower whose cup-shaped base opens into three spreading lobes. British Columbia wild ginger is 7 inches tall and has 2- to 6-inch-wide leaves. Its 1-inch brownish-purple flower opens into three lobes that develop 2-inch-long tails. European wild ginger bears glossy 2- to 3-inch wide leaves on 5-inch-tall stems; its greenish-purple flowers remain tightly cupped and are only ½ inch wide. The leaves of mottled wild ginger, up to 3 inches wide, are white-spotted, and its 2-inch-long brownish-purple flowers are splashed on the insides with violet. This species grows 8 inches tall, and its foliage turns reddish-brown in fall.

HOW TO GROW. Canada wild ginger is hardy in Zones 4-8; British Columbia, European and mottled wild ginger are hardy in Zones 4-9. They do best in open to deep shade, in a moist, well-drained humus-rich soil with a pH of 5.5 to 7.0. Plant rhizomes in spring or fall, setting them ½ inch deep, with the tip of the rhizome just reaching soil level. Space plants about 12 inches apart. Keep the soil moist throughout the year by covering it with a permanent mulch of oak or beech leaves. Propagate by dividing rhizomes in early spring or fall, except in southern areas, where they can be divided and replanted at any time as long as they are kept moist.

ASPERULA

A. gussonii (woodruff); *A. odorata,* also called *Galium odoratum* (sweet woodruff)

Woodruffs, commonly considered woodland plants, grow naturally in the rocky soil of moraines and screes, and some species thrive on sunny cliffs and are well suited to wall gardens out in the open, unshaded by trees. All of them are perennials, forming dense and sometimes invasive mats of attractive foliage. Woodruff's flowers are small but profuse, blooming in loose clusters at the ends of square stems. *A. gussonii* grows only 3 inches tall, and has very short, slender stems thickly set with whorls each composed of four shiny dark green leaves, ½ inch long. It blooms in early summer, producing pale pink tubular flowers, ¼ inch across; these are so numerous that they hide the foliage. Sweet woodruff, a somewhat larger species, forms mounds 6 to 8 inches tall; its stems are surrounded, pinwheel-fashion, by whorls of eight leaves, 1 to 2 inches long. From early to midsummer the foliage is capped by dainty clusters of star-shaped white flowers, ¼ inch across. Both flowers and foliage are sweet scented; when dried, they smell of new-mown hay and are used to flavor May wine.

HOW TO GROW. *A. gussonii* is hardy in Zones 4-7 and does best in full sun in a gravelly or sandy soil with a pH of 6.0 to 7.5; good drainage is essential. Sweet woodruff is hardy in Zones 4-9 and does best in open shade in a moist, well-drained soil with an acid pH of 4.5 to 5.5, enriched with leaf mold or peat moss. Plant woodruffs in the spring or fall, setting them about 10 to 12 inches apart. The plants will occasionally seed themselves, but for new plants it is easier to divide existing plants in the spring, just as growth begins.

ASTER
A. alpinus (alpine aster); *A. linearifolius* (savoryleaf aster, stiff aster)

Both these wild asters are found on steep, rocky slopes and do well in alpine gardens. They are slender, upright perennials with narrow, hairy leaves, 1 to 2 inches long, and daisy-like flowers that usually bloom from midsummer through fall. Alpine aster grows 6 to 9 inches tall and spreads 12 to 18 inches wide. The species bears blue to violet flowers, 1 to 2 inches wide, with deep yellow centers, but the variety Albus has white flowers, Coeruleus blue flowers, Rosea pink flowers, and Rubra reddish-purple flowers. Savoryleaf aster has tough, wiry stems, 5 to 18 inches tall, and 1-inch violet flowers. Some of the modern selections are Roseus with pink flowers, Alba with white flowers, and Purpurea with deep purple flowers.

HOW TO GROW. Alpine aster is hardy in Zones 3-8; savoryleaf aster in Zones 4-10. Both do well in full sun but tolerate partial shade. They thrive in a deep, well-drained sandy soil with a pH of 6.0 to 7.5. Sow seeds in spring and thin seedlings to stand 8 inches apart. Flowering begins in the second year. To encourage branching, snip off stem tips in the late spring and again in early summer. Propagate from seed or by dividing root clumps in fall or spring; for colored varieties, division is preferable, since plants do not always breed true from seed.

ATLAS DAISY See *Anacyclus*

AUBRIETA
A. deltoidea (purple rock cress)

One of the most charming sights in any rock garden is purple rock cress in full bloom, cascading from the crevices of an old stone wall or spreading in patches over the faces of large rocks. In addition, this versatile evergreen may be used as an edging plant at the base of a rocky slope. Purple rock cress forms a dense mound of carpet-like growth 3 to 6 inches high. Its small, downy, gray-green leaves are hidden under numerous ¾-inch flowers in spring and early summer.

The popularity of purple rock cress has prompted growers to develop many varieties in red, violet, blue and mauve as

For climate zones and frost dates, see maps, pages 150-151.

ALPINE ASTER
Aster alpinus

PURPLE ROCK CRESS
Aubrieta deltoidea

well as different shadings of the original purple. Some flower more freely; others have larger flowers or double flowers; there are varieties with golden or variegated foliage. Once established, purple rock cress spreads rapidly and may crowd out smaller, less aggressive plants if it is not pruned back.

HOW TO GROW. Purple rock cress is hardy in Zones 4-8. It grows best in full sun, but needs some shade in hot, dry areas. It does best in a sandy, well-drained soil with a pH of 6.0 to 8.0. Set plants in the ground in spring or fall, spacing them 10 inches apart. Water them occasionally during dry periods, but be careful not to overwater; excessive moisture is harmful to their foliage. After flowering, prune plants severely to control their size and to encourage a second flowering in autumn. Propagate species plants from seeds sown directly in the permanent location in spring or fall; propagate varieties from stem cuttings taken before or after the plants flower or by dividing established plants, preferably in the fall.

AURICULA PRIMROSE See *Primula*
AVENS, MOUNTAIN See *Dryas*
AZALEA See *Rhododendron*

B

BABIES'-BREATH, CREEPING See *Gypsophila*
BARRENWORT See *Epimedium*
BASKET-OF-GOLD See *Alyssum*
BEARBERRY See *Arctostaphylos*
BEARDED IRIS, DWARF See *Iris*

BELLIS
B. perennis (English daisy)

The common English daisy forms low mats of foliage that are useful for scattering throughout a rock garden or for framing paving stones. These small plants grow only 3 to 6 inches·tall, with rosettes of 1- to 2-inch slightly hairy leaves. The flowers bloom singly on short stems, just above the foliage, in masses of color—white, pink or red. They are 1 to 2 inches wide and may be single flowered, with one layer of petals, or double, with more than one layer. Two excellent miniature varieties with double blooms only ½ to 1 inch wide are Dresden China with pink flowers and Rob Roy with red flowers. There is also a double-flowered strain, Monstrosa, whose flowers are 2 inches or more wide. All English daisies have yellow centers, but the overlapping petals on double types cover this disk. In most zones, flowers bloom from early spring to early summer and sometimes again in fall, but along the California coast, the plants often flower all year long. They are short-lived perennials, so they are usually treated as biennials and are planted every other year.

HOW TO GROW. English daisies grow throughout Zones 3-10 except along the Gulf Coast. They need full sun or partial shade and do best in a moist, rich soil with a pH of 6.0 to 7.5. Set out young plants in spring, spacing smaller types 3 to 5 inches apart and larger kinds 6 to 9 inches apart. Plants may also be started from seed. In Zones 3-7 sow seeds in spring for flowers the following spring; in Zones 3-5 place seedlings in a cold frame during the winter. In Zones 8-10 sow seeds in a permanent location in late summer or early fall for flowers the following spring. For better foliage and healthier plants, snip off flowers before seeds form. In very cold climates, Zones 3-5, protect English daisies over the winter by lifting clumps and storing them in a cold frame, covering them with a 4- to 6-inch mulch of light hay. Propagate by dividing clumps in early spring or after flowering or by collecting and sowing seeds. Double-flowering types, however, cannot be

ENGLISH DAISY
Bellis perennis

102

started from the seeds of home-grown plants because they usually revert to the single-flowered type.

BIRD'S-NEST SPRUCE, SMALL See *Picea*
BISHOP'S HAT See *Epimedium*
BITTER-ROOT See *Lewisia*
BLEEDING HEART See *Dicentra*
BLUE-EYED MARY See *Omphalodes*
BLUEBELL OF SCOTLAND See *Campanula*
BOXWOOD See *Buxus*
BOXWOOD, KINGSVILLE DWARF See *Buxus*
BRITISH COLUMBIA WILD GINGER See *Asarum*
BROOM See *Cytisus*

BRUCKENTHALIA

B. spiculifolia (spike heath)

Spike heath is an evergreen shrub with branches densely covered by tiny needle-like leaves. Tucked among rocks, it spreads to create a low-growing carpet, rarely exceeding 1 foot in height. During late summer, spike heath is covered with fragrant pink bell-shaped flowers, only ⅛ inch long, blooming along flower spikes 6 inches high. As the plant spreads, its roots penetrate deeply into the ground, so it thrives in rocky soil where moisture and nutrients lie well below the surface.

HOW TO GROW. Spike heath is hardy in Zones 4-8. It grows best in full sun in a well-drained gritty or sandy soil with an acid pH between 4.5 and 6.5. Set out plants in spring, placing them where their roots will stay cool during summer, beside a rock or large stone. Work sandy peat into the planting hole to assure a vigorous root system, and water young plants regularly until they are well rooted. Once established, their deep roots make them drought resistant. In areas where winter cold is severe, protect spike heath with a cover of pine boughs. To encourage thicker foliage, snip off faded flower stalks. Propagate additional plants by rooting stem cuttings taken in the spring or by moving outer layers in spring or autumn.

BUGLEWEED See *Ajuga*
BUTTERCUP, MOUNTAIN See *Ranunculus*

BUXUS

B. microphylla 'Compacta' (Kingsville dwarf boxwood, or box)

Whether massed in large rock gardens or used as an accent in smaller gardens, the Kingsville dwarf boxwood has a neat, formal appearance. The compact mounds of glossy, dark green leaves eventually reach a height of 1 foot and a spread of 4 feet, but growth is very slow: it takes a 2-inch cutting at least five years to reach the size of a tennis ball. The leaves are oval, ½ inch long, and are generally evergreen but may discolor if exposed to severe, prolonged cold weather. Flowers on all boxwoods are inconspicuous.

HOW TO GROW. Boxwood is unable to withstand temperature extremes, hot or cold, and grows best in the moderate climates of Zones 5-9 in the eastern half of the United States, or in Zones 8 and 9 along the Pacific Coast. Give it a location with full sun or partial shade and a moist, well-drained soil enriched with peat moss or leaf mold. The soil can range from slightly acid to slightly alkaline, pH 6.0 to 7.5. Plant boxwood in spring or early fall, and keep the soil moist for several weeks after planting. In summer, place an inch-thick mulch of organic material such as leaf mold or wood chips around the plants; this keeps the soil cool and moist and also cuts down the need for weeding, a chore that may damage

SPIKE HEATH
Bruckenthalia spiculifolia

KINGSVILLE DWARF BOXWOOD
Buxus microphylla 'Compacta'

For climate zones and frost dates, see maps, pages 150-151.

LOW POPPY MALLOW
Callirhoe involucrata

SCOTCH HEATHER
Calluna vulgaris

boxwood's shallow roots. Fertilize the plants in early spring by sprinkling cottonseed meal around them and watering it in. Little pruning is necessary except to remove dead or damaged branches in spring.

The Kingsville dwarf boxwood can be propagated by rooting stem cuttings taken in the summer or early fall, though the process is time consuming. In colder areas of Zone 5, keep newly rooted cuttings in a cold frame over the winter and plant them in the garden the following spring.

C

CALLIRHOE

C. involucrata (low poppy mallow, wine cup)

A native of the dry sunny grasslands of the West, the low poppy mallow brightens a rock garden with a continuous display of deep red saucer-shaped flowers from late spring to summer's end. Its sprawling stems, up to 3 feet long, are covered with deeply cut hairy leaves, and are especially attractive carpeting a rocky slope or trailing over the face of a stone wall. The plant grows only 6 inches but it has a very long taproot, and care must be taken to provide soil sufficiently deep to accommodate it. The flowers are 2 inches wide and are borne on stems that rise from the leaf axils. Although the standard color of the flowers is rich wine red, there is also a variety, Lineariloba, whose flowers are pale blue-violet with white edges. A perennial, the low poppy mallow dies back to the crown each winter.

HOW TO GROW. The low poppy mallow is hardy in Zones 3-10. It requires a sunny location and a sandy, nearly neutral soil, pH 6.0 to 7.5. Good drainage is essential since the roots may rot in soggy soil. Set out plants in spring or fall, spacing them 18 inches apart. Propagate by sowing seeds directly in their permanent location in the spring, after danger of frost has passed, or by rooting stem cuttings taken in early summer. Except as a seedling, this plant is difficult to transplant because of its deep taproot.

CALLUNA

C. vulgaris (Scotch heather)

Scotch heather, conjuring up images of Scottish moors, is a rewarding plant for rock gardens with similar settings of bare slopes and open ground. This evergreen shrub forms neat mounds of upright stems sheathed in minute, clasping leaves ⅛ inch long. Some types are only 4 inches tall; others rise to a height of 3 feet. Throughout the summer, 6- to 10-inch flower spikes of red, pink or white cover the plants with a blanket of color.

Although there is only one species of Scotch heather, its seeds commonly do not breed true, so many different varieties have been developed. Among them are Aurea and Foxii Nana, both with purple flowers; the former is 18 inches high, the latter is a dwarf, growing only 4 inches high. Two popular pink-flowering varieties are H. E. Beale, which reaches a height of 2 feet, and J. H. Hamilton, a double-flowering form 9 inches tall. Tomentosa bears lavender flowers on plants that grow 10 inches tall.

HOW TO GROW. Scotch heather is hardy in Zones 4-8. It does best in full sun in a well-drained soil, moist but never soggy, with an acid pH of 4.5 to 6.0. A soil rich in peat moss, but not in nutrients, is recommended; heathers grow best in rather poor soil, often becoming leggy in fertile soils. Set out plants in early spring, spacing them 1 to 2 feet apart, depending on their ultimate size. Water newly planted Scotch heather during dry periods for the first year; once established, it is fairly drought-resistant. Prune the plants every spring to strengthen them and force new growth. Apply a mixture of equal parts of sand and peat moss around them each year to encourage and renew root growth, but do not cultivate around plants because their roots are very shallow. Where winters are very cold, protect plants with evergreen branches and mulch. Scotch heather is susceptible to fungus disease during moist, humid summers, but a fungicide used at the first signs of infection is effective in controlling it. Propagate Scotch heather by removing layers in the spring or by taking stem cuttings in late summer.

CAMPANULA
C. carpatica (Carpathian harebell); *C. cochleariifolia; C. rotundifolia* (bluebell of Scotland, harebell)

The huge family of campanulas includes a number of low-growing perennials suitable for planting in rock gardens and in the crevices of rock walls and flagstones. All are prized for their easy culture and profusion of richly colored, usually blue flowers, which begin to bloom in early summer and continue until fall.

The Carpathian harebell produces neat clumps of oval leaves 4 to 6 inches high. Cup-shaped flowers 1½ to 2 inches across are borne singly on wiry stems 6 to 8 inches high. Among the favored varieties are Blue Carpet, a clear medium blue; Cobalt, deep blue; Wedgewood, pale blue; and White Wedgewood, white. *C. cochleariifolia* is a creeping species that spreads on underground runners to form tufted mats 12 inches wide and 4 to 6 inches high. It has shiny oval leaves, 1 inch long, and is often grown in the alpine garden as a ground cover. Dainty bright blue bell-shaped flowers, ½ inch long, dangle above the foliage on 3-inch stems, and there is also a pure white variety, Alba.

The beloved bluebell of Scotland produces clumps 6 to 12 inches high and spreads 9 to 18 inches. It has heart-shaped lower leaves, 1 inch long, and slender upper leaves, 3 inches long. Loose clusters of drooping 1-inch-long bright blue flowers rise above the foliage on 12-inch wiry stems. This widespread campanula comes in several shades of blue, as well as a white variety, Alba.

HOW TO GROW. The Carpathian harebell is hardy in Zones 3-8, *C. cochleariifolia* in Zones 4-8 and bluebell of Scotland in Zones 2-8. All do best in full sun but will tolerate partial shade. As a group, the campanulas thrive in a moist, well-drained but fairly rich sandy or gravelly soil. *C. cochleariifolia* benefits from a soil with a pH of 6.0 to 7.0; the others will grow in a more acid soil, pH 5.0 to 7.0. Set out plants in the spring, spacing them 12 to 18 inches apart. In hot, dry climates, water during the growing season. Campanulas may be propagated from seed sown in late spring for flowers the following year or from stem cuttings of new growth taken early in the summer. But additional plants are customarily started by dividing clumps in the early spring, since the plants often benefit from division every three or four years to prevent them from becoming overcrowded.

CANADA WILD GINGER See *Asarum*
CANADIAN HEMLOCK, DWARF See *Tsuga*
CANDYTUFT See *Iberis*
CAROLINA SPRING BEAUTY See *Claytonia*
CARPATHIAN HAREBELL See *Campanula*
CARPET BUGLE See *Ajuga*
CATCHFLY, ALPINE See *Silene*
CEDAR, DWARF JAPANESE See *Cryptomeria*

CERATOSTIGMA
C. plumbaginoides, also called *Plumbago larpentiae* (leadwort)

For climate zones and frost dates, see maps, pages 150-151.

CARPATHIAN HAREBELL
Campanula carpatica

LEADWORT
Ceratostigma plumbaginoides

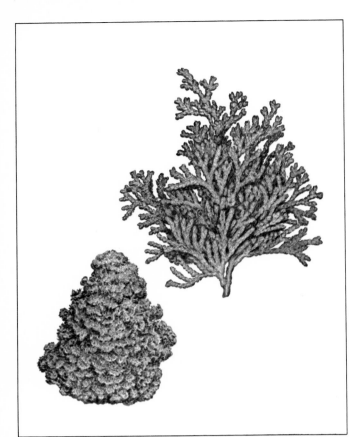

HINOKI FALSE CYPRESS
Chamaecyparis obtusa 'Nana Gracilis'

GOLDENSTAR
Chrysogonum virginianum

With its deep blue flowers and glossy green leaves, lead-wort is unexcelled as a ground cover for rock gardens. But it is equally attractive as an accent plant, grown between stones over which its branching stems can trail. It reaches a height of 9 to 12 inches, its wiry stems forming tufted mounds as much as 15 inches in diameter. The flowers are 1 inch across and appear singly or in clusters at the ends of the many branches; they bloom from late summer until frost, when few other plants provide color. Leadwort's ornamental value is also extended into fall by its oval 3½-inch leaves, which in very cold climates turn reddish-bronze.

HOW TO GROW. Leadwort is hardy in Zones 6-10. It will survive in shade but flowers more freely in a sunny, open position. A sandy, well-drained soil is essential, preferably one to which peat moss or leaf mold has been added; dormant plants cannot tolerate soggy soil. Set out plants in early spring, spacing them 18 to 24 inches apart. For winter protection in northern areas, protect plants with a 6-inch-thick mulch. Propagate by dividing plants in the spring, just as growth commences, or from stem cuttings taken in the summer. Leadwort spreads rapidly.

CHAMAECYPARIS

C. obtusa 'Nana'; *C. obtusa* 'Nana Gracilis'; *C. obtusa* 'Pygmaea' (all called Hinoki false cypress); *C. pisifera* 'Compacta' (Sawara false cypress)

Of more than 40 varieties of Japanese false cypress, these four from two species are recommended for rock gardens, being slow-growing, easily cultivated and readily available. Since these plants are often misnamed, it may be better to select specimens by their appearance rather than by their labels. Like all false cypresses, these are distinguished by flattened fan-shaped leaf sprays, with leaves that are either overlapping and scalelike or thin and needle-like. Cones are seldom more than ½ inch across, and plants may be conical, rounded or spreading, with foliage of varying colors.

Nana is an extremely slow-growing plant; it may reach no more than 6 inches in height and 8 inches in width in 10 years. The foliage is a dark, dull green, forming dense, upward-curving horizontal layers; the shrub is rounded to slightly conical in shape. Nana Gracilis is an exceptionally sturdy plant with shiny, bright green leaves and an upright cone shape. It may reach a height of 6 to 8 feet and a spread of 4 to 6 feet in 30 years. Pygmaea is a flattened, spreading specimen with large, closely spaced horizontal leaf fans. Green in summer, the plant sometimes turns bronze in fall and winter. After 10 years, it may be 18 inches tall with a spread of 24 to 30 inches. Compacta forms a dense, rounded bush with closely packed leaf sprays that curve downward. The foliage is blue-green or gray-green in summer, turning brownish-green in winter. It grows very slowly, reaching a height of 24 inches and a spread of 48 inches in 20 years.

HOW TO GROW. False cypresses are hardy in cool, moist areas of Zones 5-8. They tolerate sun but do best in partial shade. A moist, well-drained acid soil, pH 5.5 to 6.5, is ideal. Plant in spring or fall in sites protected from strong wind. Keep plants evenly moist until they are well established, about two years. Mulch dwarf plants in winter and, if winds are severe, build shelters around them. False cypresses are damaged by air pollution. Propagate additional plants from cuttings taken in the fall.

CHRYSOGONUM

C. virginianum (goldenstar)

Goldenstar, a woodland wildflower, blooms reliably in a shaded rock garden year after year, provided its surroundings are neither very moist nor extremely dry. Named for its yellow five-petaled flowers, 1½ inches wide, this perennial blooms continuously throughout summer. The flowers are borne at the tips of stiff stems that rise from a clump of foliage that reaches 1 to 2 feet in height. Its coarse, hairy leaves, 1 to 3 inches long, are toothed and oval shaped. Once goldenstar is established, it spreads eventually to cover several square feet.

HOW TO GROW. Goldenstar is hardy in Zones 4-8. It does best in light shade but will tolerate full sun if watered during dry periods. It thrives in a soil rich in leaf mold but tolerates and will flower well in any well-drained soil with a pH of 6.0 to 7.5. Set out new plants in the spring, spacing them 18 inches apart. Propagate by dividing clumps in the spring.

CHECKERBERRY See *Mitchella*
CINQUEFOIL See *Potentilla*

CLAYTONIA
C. caroliniana (Carolina spring beauty); *C. virginica* (Virginia spring beauty)

The spring beauties are woodland wildflowers that adapt easily to a cool, moist rock garden. They are prized for their delicate pink or white flowers, borne in early spring, and for their fleshy grasslike leaves. Spring beauties lose their foliage after flowering. Thus, they should be placed among companion plants that remain green through the summer. Both species are less than 1 foot high, produce flowers less than 1 inch across in loose clusters, and grow from small fleshy corms. The Virginia spring beauty has 7-inch leaves, while those of the Carolina spring beauty are shorter and broader; also, the Carolina species blooms slightly earlier than its relative.

HOW TO GROW. Spring beauties are hardy in Zones 4-8. They grow best in partial shade, in a moist, well-drained soil; a pH of 5.5 to 7.0 is recommended. Set out new plants in fall or early spring, spacing them 2 to 3 inches apart, preferably in large drifts. Propagate from fresh seeds planted in spring. Once established, the plants will seed themselves, and their seedlings can be transplanted.

COLUMBINE See *Aquilegia*
COMMON FAWN LILY See *Erythronium*
COMMON THRIFT See *Armeria*
CORNISH HEATH See *Erica*

CORYDALIS
C. bulbosa, also called *C. halleri* and *C. solida* (fumewort); *C. lutea* (yellow corydalis)

Valued for their feathery foliage and curiously shaped flowers, like those of bleeding heart, the perennial forms of corydalis are often found growing naturally in old rock walls and are recommended for either sunny or shaded areas.

The fumewort grows from a fleshy corm and blooms in early spring, producing flower spikes of 10 to 20 rose, purple or white flowers, ¾ inch long, on 8-inch stems. The blue-green foliage forms a compact rosette at the base of the plant, 8 to 10 inches across. Yellow corydalis has fibrous roots and many stems and produces a mound of gray-green foliage 12 to 18 inches high. Its ¾-inch yellow flowers bloom in loose clusters all summer long, beginning in late spring. The plant seeds itself and may become invasive if spent flowers or seedlings are not removed.

HOW TO GROW. Fumewort and yellow corydalis are hardy in Zones 4-8. They grow best in a moist, well-drained sandy or gravelly soil with a pH of 6.0 to 8.0. Set out new plants in

VIRGINIA SPRING BEAUTY
Claytonia virginica

YELLOW CORYDALIS
Corydalis lutea

For climate zones and frost dates, see maps, pages 150-151.

SAFFRON CROCUS
Crocus sativus

SPRING-FLOWERING CROCUS
Crocus versicolor

spring, spacing them 8 to 10 inches apart. To keep the roots of corydalis cool during summer, plant them where the roots will grow beneath or beside a rock or large stones. Propagate yellow corydalis from fresh seed sown directly in the garden or by transplanting volunteer seedlings while they are very small; germination may take up to two years. Fumewort can also be propagated from seed, but more commonly new plants are started from offshoots of the corms, separated in summer, after the foliage withers.

COWSLIP See *Primula*
CRANE'S-BILL See *Geranium*
CREEPING BABIES'-BREATH See *Gypsophila*
CREEPING PHLOX See *Phlox*
CRESTED GENTIAN See *Gentiana*
CRESTED IRIS See *Iris*

CROCUS

C. chrysanthus; C. sativus (saffron crocus); *C. tomasinianus; C. versicolor* (spring-flowering crocus)

A number of crocuses naturalize easily in the rock garden, forming colonies of spring or fall color. These four species grow wild on stony limestone slopes and do equally well in similar domesticated environments. They are the parents of many varieties that, although they bear the species name, may be quite unlike the species in color or form. However, all of them are small plants whose leaves and flowers rise directly from a swollen underground stem, the corm. Because their foliage dies back when the plants become dormant, they are frequently planted among such dwarf alpine plants as saxifrages, whose dense foliage hides the withering leaves of the crocuses.

C. chrysanthus blooms in early spring, its narrow gray-green leaves appearing at the same time as the yellow flowers. The leaves are about 12 inches long with prominent midribs; the flowers are cup shaped and 3 inches tall. In some varieties the flowers are deep orange, almost brown, and there are also varieties that are speckled and veined with brown and red-purple. Saffron crocus, the crocus whose flower stigma provides the world's most expensive flavoring, saffron, blooms in the fall. Its flowers and foliage appear simultaneously, and the latter stays green all winter, dying back in the spring. The 15- to 18-inch-long leaves are as slender as grass. The star-shaped flowers, 2 inches across, are usually white tinged or veined with purple, but some varieties are lilac-pink.

C. tomasinianus blooms in early spring, its leaves appearing after the flowers have opened. Its blooms are pale mauve on the outside, lilac within, and when fully open are star shaped and 3 inches wide. The narrow leaves are dark green with white midribs. Some varieties of this species are red-purple, and there is also a pure white form.

Spring-flowering crocus produces both flowers and leaves at the same time, in early spring. The flowers are creamy white streaked with purple, about 1½ inches long, and the grasslike leaves are 8 to 9 inches long.

HOW TO GROW. All four of these crocuses are hardy in Zones 5-10, but south of Zone 7 their performance is erratic, for they need cold winters to complete their growth cycle. They do best in full sun but will tolerate partial shade and thrive in a light, well-drained sandy soil enriched with leaf mold or compost. Plant corms in the fall in groups of five or more, setting them 2 to 4 inches deep and 2 to 6 inches apart. Crocuses may be lifted and separated every three or four years if desired. *C. tomasinianus* seeds itself readily but the saffron crocus is sterile. All four species may be propagated by separating and replanting offshoots of the corms after the foliage begins to turn yellow.

CROSS-LEAVED HEATH See *Erica*

CRYPTOMERIA

C. japonica 'Globosa Nana'; *C. japonica* 'Lobbii Nana'; *C. japonica* 'Vilmoriniana' (all called dwarf Japanese cedar)

The dwarf Japanese cedars are slow-growing evergreen shrubs, useful in the rock garden as specimen plants or for providing a framework against which to display small plants. Their distinguishing characteristics include thin, curving needles, ¼ inch long, clasped in spirals along the stems, and peeling reddish-brown bark.

Globosa Nana is cone shaped when it is young, but as it matures its silhouette becomes more rounded. Growing at the rate of less than 2 inches a year, it will reach a height of 18 inches in 15 years and ultimately become 3 to 6 feet high with a spread of 2 to 5 feet. The drooping, spreading branches are covered with yellow-green needles that become slightly blue in the winter.

Lobbii Nana forms a small cone-shaped tree, reaching a height of 2 to 10 feet in 10 years. It has short, compact branches with tight knots of foliage that form along the stems. The needles of this variety, straighter than those on other dwarf Japanese cedars, are light green in summer and bronze in winter.

Vilmoriniana reaches 15 inches in height and 20 inches across in 10 years. It forms a compact mound with a slightly irregular appearance, from the clumpy nature of the new growth. The closely packed leaves are light green in summer, turning reddish-purple to bronze in winter. Dwarf Japanese cedars are intolerant of polluted air.

HOW TO GROW. Vilmoriniana and Lobbii Nana are hardy in Zones 5-10, Globosa Nana in Zones 6-10. In Zones 5-7, the foliage of all three may turn brownish in winter and should be shielded from winter sun. A deep, sandy soil with a pH of 5.5 to 6.5 is recommended, and the soil should be kept evenly and constantly moist, especially when the plants are young. Plant in spring or fall. Mulch winter and summer with a 2-inch layer of organic material, such as compost or leaf mold. Pruning is seldom needed. Dwarf Japanese cedars can be transplanted easily only when young.

CYPRESS, FALSE See *Chamaecyparis*
CYPRESS, HINOKI FALSE See *Chamaecyparis*
CYPRESS, SAWARA FALSE See *Chamaecyparis*

CYTISUS

C. decumbens (prostrate broom); *C. kewensis* (Kew broom)

The brooms are odd but interesting shrubs that flourish in poor, dry soils where few other plants will grow. In the rock garden they are used to best advantage above a large rock face over which their trailing branches can sprawl. They flower profusely in spring or summer, depending on the species. Though the flowers are small, the effect is spectacular, for they bloom singly or in clusters all along the branches, and each tiny flower resembles a yellow sweet pea. The slender leaves are decorative as well, giving the plant a fine-textured appearance. And even after the leaves fall, the plant's thicket of green twigs provides color throughout the winter.

Prostrate broom produces a thick mat of foliage, 8 inches high. Its gray-green leaflets are ¾ inch long, and its flowers, which bloom in summer, are bright yellow. Kew broom has creamy white flowers, which bloom in spring, and soft hairy

DWARF JAPANESE CEDAR
Cryptomeria japonica 'Globosa Nana'

For climate zones and frost dates, see maps, pages 150-151.

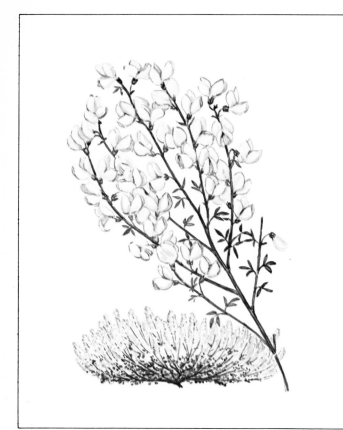

KEW BROOM
Cytisus kewensis

gray-green leaflets ¾ inch long. The plant is only a foot high but may cover an area 6 feet in diameter.

HOW TO GROW. Both prostrate and Kew broom are hardy in Zones 5-8 and grow best in full sun in dry open sites. Since these plants require perfect drainage, a soil with a high content of sand or gravel is recommended, but the pH is of no consequence. Set out plants in the spring, spacing them and taking care not to damage their sparse root systems. Brooms should be placed in a permanent site since they do not transplant well. It is necessary for newly planted shrubs to be watered during dry periods the first year, though once established they are drought resistant. Immediately after flowers have faded, prune plants to prevent them from becoming leggy or straggly. Propagate additional plants from stem cuttings taken in summer or fall.

D

DAISY, ATLAS See *Anacyclus*
DAISY, ENGLISH See *Bellis*

DAPHNE

D. arbuscula; D. cneorum (rose daphne, garland flower); *D. retusa*

Daphnes grow wild on rocky hillsides, making them a natural choice for alpine gardens. Many daphnes are small trees but these three are shrubs, and two of them are useful as creeping ground covers. Daphnes are not care-free plants, having rather exacting cultural requirements, but they reward gardeners with masses of sweetly scented spring flowers and handsome evergreen foliage. Keep in mind that all parts of the plants are poisonous if eaten.

The diminutive *D. arbuscula*, a creeping species, reaches only 6 inches in height with a spread of 2 feet. Its glossy dark green leaves are ¾ to 1 inch long, and its tiny rose-pink flowers bloom in clusters 1 to 1½ inches across. The rose daphne, most popular of all the daphnes, produces mounds of trailing branches up to 12 inches high and 2 feet across. The branches are densely clothed with narrow gray-green leaves, 1 inch long, and an abundance of extremely fragrant pink flowers borne in 1-inch clusters at the branch tips. The flowers are followed by orange berries that eventually turn brown. One variety, Exima, produces larger flowers a deeper shade of pink; another, Alba, has white flowers. There is an extremely small variety, *D. pygmaea,* that grows only 3 inches high. *D. retusa* is a compact alpine shrub, growing 2 to 3 feet high, with a spread of 1½ to 3 feet. Its pink flowers, purple inside, bloom in dense 3-inch clusters and are followed by oval red berries. The leaves are shiny above, dull beneath, and are 1 to 3 inches long.

HOW TO GROW. Rose daphne and *D. arbuscula* are hardy in Zones 4-8, *D. retusa* in Zones 6-8. They do best in full sun but will tolerate partial shade and need a sandy, well-drained soil, rich in leaf mold, with a pH of 5.5 to 7.5. Set out plants in spring, spacing them 18 inches apart. Choose a sheltered position, protected from winter winds and beside rocks where their roots will stay cool and moist throughout summer. Prune plants lightly after flowering to keep them neat and compact. Mulch well in late fall for winter protection, especially in northern areas. Mulch again in the spring with a mixture of leaf mold and sand, to renew the plants' vigor, but do not disturb their roots. Daphnes have few roots, and may easily be harmed if moved. For this reason mature plants should not be transplanted. Propagate additional plants from stem cuttings taken in late summer.

DAPHNE, OCTOBER See *Sedum*

ROSE DAPHNE
Daphne cneorum

DICENTRA

D. canadensis (squirrel corn); *D. cucullaria* (Dutchman's breeches); *D. eximia* (fringed bleeding heart); *D. formosa* (western bleeding heart, Pacific bleeding heart)

Although dicentra is most familiar as a 2-foot-tall cultivated garden perennial, there are several smaller species that are woodland wildflowers and are suited to the crevices and the limited spaces of a shaded rock garden. They too are prized for their feathery foliage and their unusual swollen flowers, which dangle rather like ladies' earrings from graceful arching stems.

Squirrel corn grows from tiny yellow tubers that look like grains of corn. Clusters of green-tinged white flowers, ½ inch long, bloom in the spring on 6- to 10-inch mounds of gray-green leaves. After flowering, the plants become dormant and lose their leaves. Therefore, they should be planted among companions that retain their foliage through the summer. Dutchman's breeches is similar to squirrel corn in foliage, size and habit of growth. The flowers, however, are different. They are white with yellow tips and resemble tiny riding jodhpurs hanging upside down. Like squirrel corn, Dutchman's breeches grow from a tuber and become dormant after flowering.

Fringed bleeding heart is noted for its long period of bloom, from spring to early fall, and for the fact that it blooms in the shade. It grows 12 to 18 inches high and bears its pink-purple flowers, ½ to ¾ inch long, in long drooping clusters above gray-green foliage. This species is occasionally found with pure white flowers. It spreads quickly from seeds that it distributes freely. Western bleeding heart is similar in appearance to fringed bleeding heart. It reaches a height of 12 to 18 inches and bears rose-pink flowers, ⅝ inch long, from late spring through early fall. Both western and fringed bleeding hearts grow from plump underground stems known as rhizomes, spreading to form large clumps.

HOW TO GROW. Squirrel corn is hardy in Zones 4-8; Dutchman's breeches and western and fringed bleeding hearts in Zones 3-8. All are woodland plants, growing best in partial shade such as that found beneath high-branching trees or tall shrubs. However, they will tolerate full sun if the soil is kept evenly and consistently moist. Ideally the soil should be well drained with a pH of 5.5 to 7.5, and should be rich in leaf mold. Set out plants in the spring, spacing them 12 inches apart. Renew soil annually by spreading leaf mold around them. Water during dry periods throughout the growing season. Propagate from fresh seeds sown in late summer or by dividing the tubers or rhizomes after plants have flowered. Plants started from seeds may take 12 months to germinate.

DOG-TOOTH FAWN LILY See *Erythronium*
DOG-TOOTH VIOLET See *Erythronium*

DRABA

D. mollissima; D. rigida, also called *D. bryoides imbricata* (rigid draba); *D. sibirica* (Siberian draba)

The drabas are diminutive plants whose natural habitats are open rocky meadows or rock crevices on high mountains, and several of them merit a place in a scree, moraine or pockets of a rock garden. Most of them are characterized by neat rosettes of tiny leaves that grow in tufts along ground-hugging stems, by plentiful flowers that bloom in dome-shaped yellow or white clusters in the spring, and by deep taproots. They are members of the mustard family and are frequently found in alpine collections. They do need, however, a place of their own, sequestered from other plants, because they can easily be crowded out by plants that are

FRINGED BLEEDING HEART
Dicentra eximia

Draba mollissima

For climate zones and frost dates, see maps, pages 150-151.

MOUNTAIN AVENS
Dryas octopetala

GRASSY BELLS
Edraianthus pumilio

larger and more vigorous. A few are annuals, but the three listed above are perennials.

D. mollissima grows an inch or two high and spreads 6 inches or more. In late spring, it bears bright yellow cross-shaped flowers, each ⅓ to ½ inch wide, with up to 18 blooms on a spike. The rigid draba forms a mosslike mound 3 to 6 inches across. Its ¼-inch leaves are shiny and stiff, giving the plant a bristly appearance. The flowers are deep golden yellow and bloom in small clusters of five to 20 blooms; the wiry stalks are 1 to 3 inches tall. Siberian draba, the most familiar of the three, is the easiest to grow. It bears loosely spaced rosettes of hairy leaves, 1 to 3 inches high, along slender, trailing stems up to 12 inches long. Its bright yellow spring flowers bloom in drooping clusters of eight to 20 flowers on stalks 6 inches tall. It sometimes blooms a second time in the autumn.

HOW TO GROW. *D. mollissima,* the rigid draba and the Siberian draba are hardy in Zones 3-8. All do best in full sun, but the Siberian draba tolerates partial shade. Drabas thrive in a well-drained gravelly soil, pH 6.0 to 7.5. Set out plants in spring, choosing a position deep enough to accommodate their long taproots; space plants 6 inches apart. To encourage new growth, add a top layer of gritty soil annually. Remove spent flower stalks to encourage more blooms. Propagate from seeds sown in spring.

DRAGON, GREEN See *Arisaema*
DRAGONROOT See *Arisaema*
DRYAD, SUENDERMANN See *Dryas*

DRYAS

D. octopetala (mountain avens); *D. suendermannii* (Suendermann dryad)

The dryads, members of the rose family, are dwarf evergreen shrubs that grow wild in the mountains above the tree line. In a rock garden they adapt to any sunny situation and are especially useful where a year-round mat of green is desired. Their shiny dark green leaves, which look like miniature oak leaves, grow densely along prostrate trailing stems that spread rapidly to cover rock contours. In spring, the dryads produce an abundance of white saucer-shaped flowers similar in appearance to wild roses; these are followed in fall by decorative seed heads that are covered with silvery silken hairs. The mountain avens is the more familiar species. Its crinkled, scalloped leaves, green above and silver beneath, are ¾ to 1 inch long, and its white flowers with yellow centers, 1½ inches wide, rise above the foliage on 2- to 4-inch stalks. The variety Minor is even more compact, with leaves and flowers half the size of the standard plant. Suendermann dryad, a hybrid, is almost identical to the mountain avens. It differs only in the color of its flower buds, yellow until they open white, and in the fact that its flowers nod on their stems.

HOW TO GROW. Dryads are hardy in Zones 2-8. They normally grow best in full sun, though strong direct sun in winter may burn the foliage. They will also grow in partial shade. They need a light, well-drained soil, with a pH of 6.0 to 7.5, preferably one with a high content of leaf mold. Water during dry periods throughout the growing season, and add a surface layer of compost annually to renew the plants' vigor. In locations exposed to strong winter sun, protect plants with pine boughs. Propagate from seeds sown as they ripen, from stem cuttings taken in the summer, or by separating small plants that grow where stems touch the ground and put down roots. Mature dryads can be transplanted, but only with difficulty.

DUTCHMAN'S BREECHES See *Dicentra*
DWARF ALBERTA SPRUCE See *Picea*
DWARF BEARDED IRIS See *Iris*
DWARF BLACK SPRUCE See *Picea*
DWARF JAPANESE CEDAR See *Cryptomeria*

E

EDELWEISS See *Leontopodium*

EDRAIANTHUS
E. pumilio; E. serpyllifolius; E. tenuifolius (all called grassy bells)

Grassy bells are low-growing deep-rooted perennials that grow wild in the Balkans and are well suited to planting in dry rock gardens and stone walls. They have open blue bell-shaped flowers that resemble those of some cultivated campanulas, to which they are related. The plants form tufted clumps, 6 to 12 inches across, and have long, trailing stems that curl up at the tips to lift the flowers above the foliage. They bloom in late spring and early summer.

E. pumilio has slightly hairy leaves that grow in a clump 2 to 3 inches high. The deep purple flowers are 1 inch wide. *E. serpyllifolius* has smooth green lance-shaped leaves, 1 inch long, that form a mat up to 6 inches high. The flowers bloom around the edges of the mat and are violet-blue with white centers; usually they are 2 inches across, but there is a variety, Major, that has larger flowers. Also popular is a pure white variety, Albus. *E. tenuifolius* produces a mat 4 to 6 inches high. Its leaves are narrow, up to 4 inches long, with bristly edges, and its small violet-blue flowers, each 1 inch long, bloom in dense clusters of six to 10 flowers each.

HOW TO GROW. Grassy bells are hardy in Zones 3-8. They grow best in full sun, in a deep, well-drained, gravelly soil, pH 6.0 to 7.5. Set out plants in the spring, spacing them 6 inches apart. Choose a location where moisture will not collect around their roots; these plants do not tolerate consistently wet soil during the winter months. Water during dry periods throughout the growing season. Propagate from seeds sown in the early spring or by dividing the plant's multiple tufts in midspring, before the flowers appear.

ENGLISH DAISY See *Bellis*
ENGLISH PRIMROSE See *Primula*

EPIMEDIUM
E. grandiflorum, also called *E. macranthum* (epimedium, bishop's hat, barrenwort)

Epimediums are excellent plants for shady rock gardens, providing colorful foliage almost all year long and, in the spring, delightful flowers. They spread on underground runners and are therefore used as a ground cover, but they may also be tucked into crevices between rocks or between the stones of a dry wall.

The species known commonly as bishop's hat grows 9 to 12 inches high and has compound leaves made up of two or three light-green heart-shaped leaflets. In the spring, when the new leaves emerge, each leaf is rimmed with a narrow margin of red; in the fall the entire leaf turns reddish-bronze. Where winter temperatures are not extreme, this colorful foliage remains on the plant all winter. The flowers, which bloom in spring, appear in loose clusters on wiry stems; they are unusual in form, having four outer sepals topped by four petal-shaped inner sepals and finally by four true petals that end in inch-long spurs. In this species each of these flower parts is a different color—the outer sepals are reddish, the inner ones purplish, the petals white. But in cultivated vari-

BISHOP'S HAT
Epimedium grandiflorum

For climate zones and frost dates, see maps, pages 150-151.

eties the coloration is different: on Rose Queen, a popular hybrid, the entire flower is crimson with white-tipped spurs; Album is pure white; Violaceum has lavender flowers.

HOW TO GROW. Bishop's hat is hardy in Zones 3-8 and grows best in shade, thriving under the protective covering of tall shrubs or high-branched trees. However, if the soil is kept moist throughout the growing season this plant will tolerate full sun. Ideally it should have a sandy, well-drained woodland soil, rich in peat moss or leaf mold, but it will also grow in soil with a high clay content. Propagate additional plants by dividing clumps in early summer.

ERICA
E. carnea (spring heath); *E. tetralix* (cross-leaved heath); *E. vagans* (Cornish heath)

With careful selection, a rock garden can have heaths in bloom almost year round. These compact woody perennials have needle-like evergreen foliage, long-lasting flowers and masses of fibrous roots that are effective in preventing soil erosion. They spread slowly and are tolerant of both wind and salt spray. In the rock garden they are useful either as specimen plants or in massed displays, their bell-shaped blooms of white, red, pink and purple rising in tight clusters on thin, wiry stems.

Spring heath has ¼-inch leaves that may be green, bronze or yellow, depending on the variety. The creeping stems fill an area 2 to 3 feet across, forming a carpet 12 inches deep. The ¼-inch flowers often cluster on one side of the stem. In warm climates, the flowers begin to open in winter, but in northern zones they do not appear until early spring. Among varieties of special interest are Aurea, with yellow leaves and pink flowers; Eileen Porter, a long-flowering carmine variety; and King George, with rose to crimson flowers that bloom very early. Dwarf heaths that grow less than 8 inches tall include Vivellii, with vivid red flowers and leaves that turn reddish-green in winter; Snow Queen, with white flowers; and Silberschmeltze, also with white flowers, but trailing in its habit of growth.

Cross-leaved heath has fuzzy gray-green leaves only ⅛ inch long and grows 9 to 18 inches tall with a spread of up to 24 inches. The 1- to 2-inch-long clusters of ¼-inch flowers are produced throughout the summer and into fall. Varieties recommended include L. E. Underwood, with pink-brown buds that open to an apricot shade, and Mollis, with gray-white leaves and white flowers.

Cornish heath forms rounded masses 12 to 18 inches tall and equally wide. It has ⅜-inch bright green leaves, and sprays of ⅛-inch flowers, 5 to 9 inches long, that bloom from summer through fall. Varieties of this species include Grandiflora, which produces a profusion of pink blooms; Mrs. D. F. Maxwell, with deep cherry-pink flowers; and Nana, a white-flowered dwarf only 6 inches tall.

HOW TO GROW. Spring and Cornish heaths are hardy in Zones 5-7, cross-leaved heath in Zones 4-7. For abundant flowers they require full sun, but heaths will tolerate partial shade. They do best in a moist, well-drained, sandy soil enriched with peat moss or leaf mold. An acid pH of 4.5 to 5.5 is recommended, but spring heath will tolerate more neutral conditions. Plant in spring or fall. Mass plants in groups of at least six, spacing them 12 inches apart. Keep the soil evenly moist while the plants are young, and mulch with evergreen boughs, straw or dried leaves. In the spring, scatter a mixture of sand and peat moss or leaf mold around each plant. Propagate from stem cuttings taken in the summer or fall and kept over the winter in a cold frame. Or start new plants by dividing rooted prostrate stems in the spring.

CROSS-LEAVED HEATH
Erica tetralix

ERIGERON
E. aureus; E. compositus; E. uniflorus (all called fleabane)

Found growing in the rocky terrain of mountains in North America and Europe, these three low-growing fleabanes are choice plants for a sunny rock-garden situation—on a slope, in a moraine, or tucked into a rock wall. All of them are perennials, producing daisy-like flowers in the spring or summer. *E. aureus* is a creeping plant that spreads on fibrous roots, sending up 2- to 6-inch-tall tufts of hairy 3-inch leaves to form clumps 9 inches across. The leaves are almost round and spoon shaped, and they often have violet-colored stems. From spring until midsummer the mat of green foliage is dotted with ¾-inch yellow-orange flowers borne individually on 3- to 5-inch stems. *E. compositus* forms dense 3- to 6-inch-tall mounds of finely divided fuzzy gray-green leaves that spread into clumps 8 inches across. Growing from a thick taproot, this species bears white, pale blue or pink flowers with yellow centers from early summer until frost; the flowers, up to ¾ inch across, top 3- to 6-inch flower stems. *E. uniflorus* grows only 2 to 3 inches high and spreads to form dense clumps 9 inches across. The leaves have woolly surfaces and stems, and the flowers, appearing from spring until frost, are ⅝ inch across; they open white but change to lavender-blue with age.

HOW TO GROW. Fleabanes are hardy in Zones 3-8 and generally require a hot, dry, sunny location, although *E. aureus* will tolerate partial shade. They need a well-drained sandy, gritty or gravelly soil with a pH of 6.0 to 7.5. Set out plants in the fall or spring, spacing them 6 to 9 inches apart. To prolong flowering, remove faded blooms. Propagate from seeds sown in the spring, from cuttings taken in the summer or by dividing large clumps in early spring or after flowering.

ERYTHRONIUM
E. americanum (common fawn lily, yellow adder's-tongue, trout lily); *E. dens-canis* (dog-tooth violet, dog-tooth fawn lily); *E. hendersonii* (Henderson fawn lily); *E. revolutum* (mahogany fawn lily)

The nodding flowers of the fawn lilies carpet woodlands during the spring and are best used in naturalized rock gardens, either massed or planted in small clumps. The 1- to 3-inch lily-like flowers bloom on slender stems up to 12 inches tall. They have six flaring petals that curve back toward the base, in colors ranging from white to pink, rose, purple or yellow. At the base of each flower stalk are two strap-shaped leaves, which may be plain green or mottled with gray or maroon. Fawn lilies are perennials that grow from small corms. The deciduous foliage dies back to the ground by midsummer, when the plants become dormant.

The common fawn lily grows 4 to 10 inches high. Its leaves, up to 6 inches in length, are dappled with gray or brownish-purple markings; its flowers, 1½ to 2 inches long, are bright yellow suffused on the outside with reddish-brown.

The dog-tooth violet has 4- to 6-inch-long leaves mottled with gray or reddish-brown. The slightly fragrant 1- to 2-inch flowers are red, rose or purple with red markings at the base of each petal. Among the numerous named varieties are Pink Perfection, Purple King, Rose Beauty, Rose Queen and Snowflake. Also popular is the Japanese species *E. japonicum,* which has violet-to-purple flowers with black centers.

The Henderson fawn lily grows wild on the West Coast but adapts to East Coast gardens. Its 4- to 8-inch-long mottled leaves have wavy edges, and its flowers, 1½ inches long, are lavender-purple with dark purple center markings. As many as four flowers may develop on one stalk.

The mahogany fawn lily has 8-inch-long leaves with simi-

FLEABANE
Erigeron compositus

COMMON FAWN LILY
Erythronium americanum

For climate zones and frost dates, see maps, pages 150-151.

DOG-TOOTH VIOLET
Erythronium dens-canis

GALAX
Galax aphylla

lar wavy edges; they are mottled with light brown or white. The flowers, up to 2 inches long, may be white, rose-pink or lavender with darker markings but as they age they become purple. Several flowers are borne on each flower stalk, and the petals of mahogany fawn lily are more prominently curved than those of the other varieties. Recommended varieties include Albiflorum, White Beauty and Pink Beauty.

HOW TO GROW. Common fawn lily and dog-tooth violet are hardy in Zones 3-9, Henderson fawn lily and mahogany fawn lily in Zones 5-9. They all do best in the open shade of a deciduous woodland environment, and thrive in a well-drained sandy soil. Ideally the soil should be enriched with peat moss or leaf mold and have an acid to neutral pH of 5.0 to 7.0. Plant fawn lilies in groups late in the summer or in early fall. Set them 3 to 5 inches deep and space them 4 to 6 inches apart. Feed annually each spring with a light sprinkling of bone meal. Protect in winter with a mulch of coarse peat moss, chopped leaves, well-rotted manure or leaf mold.

Fawn lilies may spread by means of offsets, and a planting will last for many years. The corms can be dug up and the offsets removed and planted elsewhere if desired, but fawn lilies do not survive transplanting well, as their corms dry out quickly. They should be out of the ground for the shortest possible time, and they should be moved only after the flowers fade, as the leaves are dying down. Additional fawn lilies can also be propagated from seeds sown as soon as they are ripe. However, seeds can take up to two years to germinate, and another three years may pass before the plants produce any flowers.

EUROPEAN WILD GINGER See *Asarum*
EUROPEAN WOOD ANEMONE See *Anemone*
EVERGREEN CANDYTUFT See *Iberis*
EWERS STONECROP See *Sedum*

F
FALSE CYPRESS See *Chamaecyparis*
FAN COLUMBINE See *Aquilegia*
FAWN LILY See *Erythronium*
FLEABANE See *Erigeron*
FRINGED BLEEDING HEART See *Dicentra*
FUMEWORT See *Corydalis*

G
GALAX
G. aphylla, also called *G. urceolata* (galax, wandflower)

Galax is at its best massed on the shaded slopes of a rocky woodland garden or planted as a ground cover among rhododendrons and azaleas. The rapidly spreading underground stems, or rhizomes, quickly carpet an area with thin, shiny, leathery leaves. These are heart-shaped with toothed edges and may be as much as 5 inches across; each leaf is borne on a stiff, wiry stem, up to 9 inches long, that rises directly from the root. The evergreen leaves change to a deep bronze in fall and winter months except when grown in very deep shade. Galax bears spikes of small white flowers that bloom from late spring to midsummer on slender stalks 12 to 18 inches tall. Leaves are long lasting when cut and formerly were used in corsages and flower arrangements.

HOW TO GROW. Galax is hardy in Zones 3-8 and does best in partial shade. It will also grow in full shade. A cool, moist, well-drained woodland soil enriched with peat moss or leaf mold is ideal, preferably one with a very acid pH of 4.5 to 5.5. Keep the soil moist during the growing season and, in Zones 3 and 4, protect plants during the winter with a layer of pine boughs. Plant the thick pink rhizomes in early spring or fall, laying each piece horizontally with a bud facing up; space the pieces 6 to 12 inches apart and cover them with 1 inch of soil. Although galax may be propagated from seeds sown in a cold frame in the fall, the preferable method is to dig up and divide the rhizomes in early spring when they are dormant or in the fall when growth is mature. Make sure each rhizome piece has at least one bud.

GARLAND FLOWER See *Daphne*
GENTIAN See *Gentiana*

GENTIANA

G. acaulis (stemless gentian); *G. scabra* (rough gentian); *G. septemfida* (crested gentian)

One of the most coveted of rock-garden plants, the gentian comes in hundreds of species and hybrids, most having intensely blue trumpet-shaped flowers. The blues vary in shade from light to dark and may be turquoise or almost purple. In addition, there are gentians with white, yellow, gold or red flowers. Some varieties bloom in spring, others in summer or fall, and they range from low creepers to tall, open plants with arching stems. There is also considerable difference in their cultivation: some are easy to grow, others extremely difficult. The three species described here are alpine plants, suitable for use on shaded, stony slopes or between the rocks of dry walls or paving; they can also be grown in a cool alpine greenhouse. All three are perennials and form dense clumps.

Stemless gentian is spring flowering; in bloom, the plants are covered with upward-facing deep blue flowers, 2 to 3 inches across, marked with green or white throats. The shiny leaves, 1 inch long and ½ inch wide, spread on underground stems to form thick mats up to 18 inches across. Among the varieties of this gentian is one with white flowers, Alba, and a plant with 4-inch flowers, Gigantea. Sometimes the stemless gentian will not bloom, or blooms once and never again, for an unknown reason. The rough gentian has fall-blooming dark blue bell-shaped flowers clustered at the tips of stiff, upright stems. Its leaves are oval, 2 to 3 inches long, with rough edges. Normally this gentian is 12 inches tall and its flowers are 1 to 1¼ inches long, but the variety Buergeri grows 3 feet tall and has 2½-inch flowers.

The summer-flowering crested gentian, among the easiest to grow, bears small clusters of 1- to 2-inch-long bell-shaped blue flowers with white throats. The leafy stems grow 9 to 18 inches tall and form clumps 12 to 15 inches across; the leaves are oval, 1 to 1½ inches long. Some varieties are lower growing or have round or heart-shaped leaves, and one variety, Hascombensis, has large clusters of six to eight clear blue flowers, 2 to 3 inches long.

HOW TO GROW. Stemless gentian is hardy in Zones 3-8; crested gentian and rough gentian in Zones 4-8. Plants do best where summers are cool and moist, as in the Pacific Northwest. They generally need partial shade but tolerate full sun in cool summers, provided the soil is kept constantly moist. The ideal soil is a moist, gritty, well-drained loam enriched with peat moss or leaf mold, with a pH of 5.5 to 7.0. Plant gentians in the spring, spacing them 10 to 12 inches apart; be sure to firm the roots in the soil. Fertilize plants in spring with a light sprinkling of bone meal, dried cow manure or 5-10-10 fertilizer. Propagate stemless and crested gentians from seed sown when ripe, in late summer or fall, wintering young plants in a cold frame; for rough gentian, sow seed in the spring. Plants usually begin flowering in two years. Gentians may also be started from stem cuttings taken in the spring, wintered in a cold frame and

STEMLESS GENTIAN
Gentiana acaulis

For climate zones and frost dates, see maps, pages 150-151.

planted outdoors the following spring. Clumps may be divided in early spring or, in the case of the stemless gentian, in summer or fall after flowering.

GERANIUM
G. dalmaticum; G. renardii; G. sanguineum; G. sanguineum prostratum, also called *G. lancastriense* (all called crane's-bill)

Not to be confused with the common geranium *(Pelargonium),* crane's-bills belong to a different genus with hundreds of species, ranging from 4 inches to 2½ feet tall. The four listed here can be grown along the tops of rocky ledges, among the rocks of a dry wall or paving, as a ground cover for a rocky bank, in a moraine, or in containers in an alpine house. All are perennials that die to the ground in winter; they have divided leaves and bowl-shaped five-petaled flowers that bloom through the summer months.

G. dalmaticum forms low, dense carpets 3 to 6 inches tall, with a spread of 8 to 12 inches. The dark, glossy leaves are divided into five leaflets. In the fall, the foliage turns red. The inch-wide flowers, pink with red veins, are borne in delicate sprays on 6-inch stems. There is also a white variety. *G. renardii* grows in clumps 9 to 12 inches tall and 12 to 15 inches wide. The hairy, rounded gray-green leaves have bumpy surfaces and scalloped edges. Open clusters of inch-wide flowers may be pink, white or lavender with prominent reddish-violet veins.

G. sanguineum, a favorite garden perennial, forms dense mounds 12 inches tall and 24 inches across. The finely divided foliage turns red in the fall. The reddish-purple flowers are 1 to 2 inches wide. There is also a white variety. *G. sanguineum prostratum,* only 4 to 6 inches tall, spreads to a width of 18 inches. Its trailing stems form a thick mat on the ground. The finely textured leaves also turn red in the fall; 1-inch-wide flowers are pale pink with red veins.

HOW TO GROW. *G. dalmaticum, G. sanguineum* and *G. sanguineum prostratum* are hardy in Zones 4-10; *G. renardii* can be grown in Zones 7-10. These geraniums grow best in full sun but will tolerate partial shade. A well-drained sandy or gritty soil with poor to average fertility is best; plants tend to become rampant if the soil is too rich. A pH of 6.0 to 7.5 suits them. Geraniums can be planted in the fall or spring. Once established, they need little attention and should not be disturbed; divide them every fourth year only if the plants seem to be deteriorating.

Renew surface mulch of granite chips each fall and let the soil dry slightly between thorough waterings. *G. sanguineum* should be trimmed back to half its height after the first main flowering period to encourage branching. Propagate from seeds sown in the spring or fall, from cuttings taken in late summer, or by dividing the clumps in early spring or after flowering. Plants will often seed themselves.

GEUM
G. borisii (Boris avens), *G. reptans* (avens, geum)

Forming neat mounds of foliage and bearing large flowers that resemble strawberry blossoms, these avens can be planted in raised beds, an alpine garden or among the rocks of a retaining wall. Their brightly colored flowers appear from spring to midsummer. The foliage of Boris avens is green with a coarse texture. Each heart-shaped leaf is deeply indented. Tufts of foliage are 9 to 12 inches tall, with a spread of 12 to 15 inches. The nodding yellow to orange-red flowers are 1½ inches across and are borne on 6- to 12-inch stalks. Toothed leaflets give the foliage of *G. reptans* a delicate, fernlike texture. It grows 4 to 6 inches tall and may spread

CRANE'S-BILL
Geranium sanguineum

15 inches by long, red runners. The flowers are golden yellow and 1½ inches wide. Each flower stalk produces a single flower that later forms a wispy gray seed head.

HOW TO GROW. Both of these avens are hardy in Zones 3-8. In hot climates, midday shade is necessary; elsewhere full sun is tolerated. The soil should be a deep, well-drained, gritty loam enriched with peat moss or leaf mold, with an acid-to-neutral pH of 5.5 to 7.0. Soil must not be allowed to become dry. Plant avens in spring or fall, spacing them 10 to 12 inches apart. Sprinkle bone meal lightly around the plants in spring. To prolong the flowering period, remove flowers as they fade. A light mulch of straw, salt hay or evergreen boughs will protect plants in winter. Propagate by sowing seeds in spring, with the seedling plants being set outdoors in the fall. Or clumps may be dug and divided in early spring or fall; plants grow best when divided every two or three years. The small plantlets on runners of *G. reptans* can be detached during the summer and transplanted.

GINGER, WILD See *Asarum*
GOLDEN GARLIC See *Allium*
GOLDENSTAR See *Chrysogonum*
GRAPE HYACINTH See *Muscari*
GRASSY BELLS See *Edraianthus*
GREEN DRAGON See *Arisaema*
GROUND PINK See *Phlox*

GYPSOPHILA

G. cerastioides (mouse-ear gypsophila); *G. repens* (creeping babies'-breath); *G. tenuifolia*

Although much smaller than the usual 2- to 3-foot mounds of babies'-breath found in perennial borders, these species, better suited to rock gardens, have the same delicate cloud-like quality with tiny white or pink flowers. Deciduous perennials, they can be planted in crevices of dry walls or paving, used as an edging or allowed to trail over ledges, steps or rocks. The roots, thick and fleshy, run deep into the soil. Stems that creep above ground form spreading mats.

Mouse-ear gypsophila has small, rounded leaves that are soft, fuzzy and gray. The foliage rosettes grow 2 to 3 inches tall with a spread of 12 to 18 inches. From late spring until fall frost, clusters of flowers are borne on 3-inch stems above the foliage. The ⅛- to ½-inch-wide flowers are white with red-purple veins.

The thin, wirelike stems of creeping babies'-breath branch and rebranch to form mounds 3 to 6 inches tall and up to 2 feet across. Its narrow leaves are less than 1 inch long and are a soft gray-green color. Fast growing, it is best used in clumps cascading over rocks or walls. Graceful, open flower clusters appear throughout the summer. Only ⅓ inch wide, the flowers may be white or pink. Named varieties include Fratensis with pink flowers, Rosy Veil with double pink or white flowers and more upright growth, and Bodgeri with double pink flowers. Fine-textured *G. tenuifolia* has hairy gray-green leaves that are only ⅜ inch long. Clumps of wiry stems form mounds 8 inches tall. The white or pink flowers are ¾ inch wide.

HOW TO GROW. Mouse-ear gypsophila is hardy in Zones 5-8 and in the West Coast portions of Zone 9. Creeping babies'-breath and *G. tenuifolia* are hardy in Zones 3-8. Gypsophilas grow best in full sun but tolerate partial shade, especially the mouse-ear species. Set plants in a deep, well-drained, gravelly soil. Creeping babies'-breath and *G. tenuifolia* need soil with a pH of 6.0 to 7.5, while mouse-ear gypsophila does better in an acid soil, pH 5.5 to 6.5. Soil should be allowed to dry somewhat between waterings, but

AVENS
Geum reptans

CREEPING BABIES'-BREATH
Gypsophila repens 'Fratensis'

For climate zones and frost dates, see maps, pages 150-151.

water deeply during droughts. Plant young gypsophilas in fall or early spring, spacing them 12 to 15 inches apart. Shear plants lightly after the first major period of bloom to encourage more blooms later. Divide mouse-ear gypsophila in early spring or fall. Take cuttings of creeping babies'-breath in spring for planting outdoors in the fall. Both creeping babies'-breath and *G. tenuifolia* can easily be propagated from seeds gathered when they are ripe.

H

HAREBELL See *Campanula*
HAREBELL, CARPATHIAN See *Campanula*
HEATH See *Erica*
HEATH, SPIKE See *Bruckenthalia*
HEATHER, SCOTCH See *Calluna*

HELIANTHEMUM

H. nummularium (sun rose); *H. oelandicum alpestre,* also called *H. alpestre*

Grown for the brilliantly colored buttercup-like flowers that cover trailing, hairy foliage throughout the spring and summer, helianthemums can be used to trail over a retaining wall, to cover banks or to form an edging along a raised bed. Helianthemums can also be grown in an alpine greenhouse. These shrubby perennials are semievergreen to evergreen and are slow to become established. However, sprawling branches root where they touch the soil and in time they can overgrow other plants.

The sun rose grows up to 12 inches tall and spreads up to 36 inches wide. The narrow oval leaves are 1 inch long and are glossy dark green or gray-green, depending on the variety. The underside is gray and hairy. Clusters of 1-inch paper-thin flowers appear at the end of each trailing stem. Although each flower is short lived, hundreds are produced. There are many named varieties in a multitude of colors. The flowers may be single or double. *H. oelandicum alpestre* forms a more compact clump, with a height of 3 to 6 inches and a spread of 12 inches. The twiggy growth is covered with hairy green leaves ⅜ inch long. The flowers of this species are yellow, ¼ to ¾ inch wide.

HOW TO GROW. Helianthemums are hardy in Zones 5-9. They must have full sun to thrive. They grow best in an unfertile, dry, gravelly or sandy soil that is deep and has a pH of 7.5 to 8.5. They are difficult to transplant; purchase young plants growing in pots. Plant in early spring, spacing them 12 to 18 inches apart. Fertilize sparingly with a light sprinkling of bone meal and ground limestone in the spring. In Zones 5 and 6, mulch in the autumn with evergreen boughs. Prune the sun rose back to two thirds of the original height after the first heavy flowering to stimulate repeated bloom. The plant should also be pruned in the early spring to keep its growth bushy.

Pinch back rooted cuttings as they develop to force them to branch. Propagate helianthemums by dividing plants or sowing seeds in the spring. Cuttings of new growth can be rooted in the summer; grow these in individual pots over winter in a cold frame, setting them out the following spring. Helianthemums are not long lived and new plants should be started to replace old ones every four years.

HEMLOCK, CANADIAN DWARF See *Tsuga*
HENDERSON FAWN LILY See *Erythronium*

HEPATICA

H. americana, also called *H. triloba* (round-lobed hepatica); *H. nobilis; H. transsilvanica* (all called hepatica, liverleaf)

SUN ROSE
Helianthemum nummularium

HEPATICA
Hepatica americana

A harbinger of spring throughout open woodlands, hepaticas are best grown on rocky slopes. They may also be planted among the rocks of retaining walls or in raised beds. The semievergreen foliage remains attractive into the winter months. The three- to five-lobed leaves form dense 4- to 9-inch clumps. The bowl-shaped anemone-like flowers may be white, blue, pink or purple. The flowers, ½ to 1½ inches wide, appear in early spring on hairy stems rising above the foliage of the previous year. As the flowers fade, leathery new leaves appear. Very early in spring the ½- to 1-inch lilac to pinkish-white flowers of *H. americana* make their appearance. The plant has rounded leaf lobes and hairy stems and buds and grows 6 inches tall. *H. nobilis* grows 4 to 9 inches tall with a spread of 9 to 12 inches. The leaves have oval lobes, purplish underneath with fine, silky hairs. The 1-inch flowers are borne on 6-inch stems. Most often the flowers are blue. *H. transsilvanica* grows 4 to 6 inches tall and has a spread of 10 inches. The leaves have scalloped, toothed edges. This species is very similar to *H. nobilis* but is slightly more delicate in growth habit. The blue flowers may be up to 1½ inches across.

HOW TO GROW. Hepaticas are hardy throughout Zones 3-8. Provide open shade with some direct sun. The soil should be a gravelly woodland loam enriched with peat moss or leaf mold and having a pH of 6.0 to 7.0. The soil must be kept constantly moist. In early spring or fall, set out plants 8 to 12 inches apart. Provide winter protection by lightly mulching with leaves before the first frost; remove early the following spring. Hepaticas may be divided in the fall, keeping two or three plants in each clump. Seeds may be sown as soon as they are ripe, or in the fall to germinate the following spring.

HIMALAYAN PRIMROSE See *Primula*
HINOKI FALSE CYPRESS See *Chamaecyparis*
HOLLY, HELLER JAPANESE See *Ilex*
HORNRIM SAXIFRAGE See *Saxifraga*

HUTCHINSIA
H. alpina (alpencress)

As its name implies, alpencress is a plant for an alpine rock garden or for crevices between the stones of a dry wall or terrace. It is an evergreen perennial that forms dense low mounds of shiny smooth dark green leaves. Finely divided and feathery in appearance, these leaves are only 1 inch long and grow in a rosette 2 to 4 inches tall with a spread of 8 inches. The flowers bloom from spring through summer, covering the entire plant with 1-inch clusters of small pure white four-petaled flowers.

HOW TO GROW. Alpencress is hardy in Zones 4-8. It does best in partial shade but tolerates full sun provided temperatures are cool. Ideally it should have a well-drained gritty or gravelly soil with a pH of 6.0 to 7.5. The soil should be kept constantly moist. In areas that have intermittent snow cover, mulch in winter with evergreen boughs, straw or salt hay. Plant alpencress in spring or fall, spacing it at 3- to 6-inch intervals. Propagate from divisions in early spring or fall, from cuttings taken in summer, or from seeds sown as soon as they are ripe. Winter young plants in a cold frame.

HYACINTH, GRAPE See *Muscari*

HYPERICUM
H. calycinum (Aaronsbeard St.-John's-wort); *H. olympicum* (Olympic St.-John's-wort)

St.-John's-wort is often a large shrub, but these two species are low-growing ground covers. Commonly used on embank-

ALPENCRESS
Hutchinsia alpina

AARONSBEARD ST.-JOHN'S-WORT
Hypericum calycinum

For climate zones and frost dates, see maps, pages 150-151.

ments to control erosion, they grow vigorously and rapidly by means of creeping underground stems called stolons. In rock gardens they are suited to areas where their roots will be naturally restricted, or to the crevices of dry walls or paving stones, moraine or scree. The Olympic St.-John's-wort can also be grown in pots in a cool alpine greenhouse. St.-John's-worts are distinctive plants, often with winged or angular stems. In summer and early fall they are adorned with golden yellow five-petaled flowers centered with a star-burst of stamens. The foliage of both plants may stay green all winter, or it may turn purple-brown, depending on the severity of the weather.

Aaronsbeard St.-John's-wort, the larger of these two species, grows 12 to 18 inches tall and spreads indefinitely. Its leathery bright green oval leaves are 2 to 4 inches long, and it bears 2- to 3-inch flowers, singly or in clusters, over a long period. Olympic St.-John's-wort also grows 12 to 18 inches tall but spreads only 12 inches. Its narrow oval leaves are ½ to 1½ inches long and gray-green. It blooms profusely, bearing 1½- to 2½-inch flowers singly or in clusters. The variety Citrinum has pale yellow flowers.

HOW TO GROW. St.-John's-wort is hardy in Zones 5-8, although in the colder areas plants tend to be short-lived. Olympic St.-John's-wort in particular needs a protected location to do well. Both plants produce more flowers in full sun, but Aaronsbeard St.-John's-wort can also be grown in partial shade. Give either of these species a moist, well-drained sandy loam with a pH of 6.0 to 7.5; poor, dry soils are tolerated, but plants do not thrive. Set out plants in spring or fall, spacing Aaronsbeard St.-John's-wort 12 to 18 inches apart, Olympic St.-John's-wort 8 to 12 inches apart. A light layer of compost may be applied in autumn. In Zones 5 and 6 protect the plants with a winter mulch of evergreen boughs or salt-marsh hay. Prune as necessary, after flowering, but only to keep plants the desired shape and size. Once established, St.-John's-wort should not be disturbed unless plants become crowded, or for propagation purposes they may be divided in early spring or autumn. Cuttings of both species can be taken in early summer and held over the winter in a cold frame for planting outdoors the following spring. Plants can also be propagated from seed.

I

IBERIS

I. saxatilis (rock candytuft); *I. sempervirens* (evergreen candytuft)

The ground-hugging candytufts are mainstays of a rock garden. They are easy to grow, generally stay green the year round, and at their peak in the spring they are covered with dazzling white flowers. They can be used in the crevices of walls, among paving stones or in drifts over and around rocks. In addition, rock candytuft can be grown in pots in an alpine greenhouse.

Rock candytuft forms a 3- to 6-inch carpet of twisted, contorted branches that spread over an area 8 to 12 inches wide. It is covered with tiny, cylindrical leaves, ¾ inch long, that are a dull, dark green. The small white flowers bloom in flat-topped clusters, 2 inches across.

Evergreen candytuft spreads slowly to form a dense, compact carpet, 24 inches across, its stems rooting where they touch moist soil. It grows 6 to 12 inches tall and has shiny dark green leaves, 1 to 2 inches long. Blooming profusely into early summer, the small flowers are borne in flat clusters 2 inches across. In warmer regions, blooms may appear again in the fall. There are numerous varieties: those growing 6 to 7 inches tall include Little Gem and Purity, both with larger

EVERGREEN CANDYTUFT
Iberis sempervirens 'Snowflake'

flowers; Autumn Snow and Christmas Snow, which bloom in both spring and fall; and Snowflake, 12 inches high, with a more spreading habit of growth. There is also a pygmy candytuft that is only 4 inches tall.

HOW TO GROW. Rock candytuft is hardy in Zones 3-8, evergreen candytuft in Zones 4-8. In areas with cold winters and little snow cover, the leaves may turn brown, but fresh new growth is produced when the plants are trimmed back. Both species do best in a location with full sun or very open shade. Evergreen candytuft thrives in a well-drained sandy loam with a pH of 6.0 to 7.5; rock candytuft should be planted in scree or in any well-drained gravelly soil with a similar pH. Although both plants suffer if moisture sits around their roots, especially in winter, they should be watered regularly during prolonged droughts. Set out plants in late spring or eary fall, spacing them 6 to 18 inches apart, depending on their ultimate size. To prevent winter burn in cold areas, cover the plants with evergreen boughs. To encourage continuous new growth, prune off one third to one half of the old flower stems after the flowers fade. Renew soil every spring by working equal parts of leaf mold or peat moss, fresh soil and sand into the topsoil around the plants. Propagate from seeds, which germinate in two weeks, or from cuttings taken in the summer.

ILEX
I. crenata 'Helleri'; *I. crenata* 'Dwarf Pagoda'; *I. crenata* 'Green Dragon' (all called Japanese holly)

The dwarf forms of Japanese holly are useful as accent plants in a rock garden, placed midway down a boulder-strewn embankment or along its base. They are dense, compact shrubs with shiny dark evergreen foliage. Unlike other hollies, the small leaves are oval to round in shape and have shallow teeth rather than spines.

The Heller Japanese holly is a flat-topped plant with stiffly spreading horizontal branches; it grows 2 to 3 feet tall and 3 or more feet across. The scalloped-edged oval leaves, ¼ to ¾ inch long, are bright green. Dwarf Pagoda, the smallest of the Japanese dwarf hollies, grows only 6 to 12 inches tall and 15 inches wide. Its ¼-inch oval leaves hug the thick branches tightly, and the plant's stiff stems give it an angular appearance. The berries are so tiny they are hardly noticeable. Green dragon is the male counterpart to Dwarf Pagoda, bearing no berries. It grows slightly larger, reaching a height of 20 inches, and has a column-like shape.

HOW TO GROW. Dwarf Japanese hollies are hardy in Zones 5-8. They do well in both full sun and partial shade, and thrive in a moist, well-drained sandy soil, pH 5.5 to 6.5, enriched with ample organic matter. Set them out in the spring at the same depth as they grew in the container. Keep the young plants well watered to prevent their roots from drying; mist plants if they begin to lose leaves. Do not fertilize until one year after planting. Water Japanese hollies well during periods of drought, and mulch them with an organic material such as compost or shredded leaves to keep the roots cool and moist in summer. In the fall, allow the soil to become somewhat dry to harden the plant for the winter. In some locations it may be necessary to protect plants from drying winds and sun during the winter with a covering of evergreen boughs. The Japanese hollies maintain their shape without pinching or pruning.

IRIS
I. cristata (crested iris); *I. gracilipes* (slender iris); *I. pumila* (dwarf bearded iris); *I. verna* (vernal iris)

With hundreds of varieties to choose from, there are irises

JAPANESE HOLLY
Ilex crenata 'Dwarf Pagoda'

VERNAL IRIS
Iris verna

For climate zones and frost dates, see maps, pages 150-151.

suitable for rock gardens of every kind and size. Some thrive in sun, others in shade. All are perennials, blooming in late spring or early summer. They grow from fleshy rhizomes and have sword-shaped foliage. The clear, vivid colors of iris blooms include pink, lilac, purple, white, cream, yellow, brown, maroon, orange, black and blue; the flowers of many varieties are bicolored.

The crested iris grows 4 to 9 inches tall and will spread to cover a large area, its rhizomes forming a mat over the surface of the ground. Its flowers are lavender, 2 to 2½ inches across, with white crests marked with orange tips. The bright green broad, arching leaves die to the ground in the winter. The slender iris grows 6 to 10 inches tall. Its delicate grasslike leaves, shiny and dark green, die back in winter. The slender, branched stems bear several pinkish-lilac flat-petaled flowers, 1 to 2 inches across.

The dwarf bearded iris, suitable for a cool alpine green-house as well as a rock garden, is only 4 to 10 inches tall. It has blue-gray leaves and dark red-purple flowers. The vernal iris forms spreading clumps of shiny evergreen foliage, 3 to 10 inches tall. Because the flower stems are so short, the blooms seem to nestle among the foliage. The fragrant flowers, up to 3 inches across, may be purple or white.

HOW TO GROW. The crested iris is hardy in Zones 3-8, the dwarf bearded iris in Zones 4-8, the slender iris in Zones 5-8 and the vernal iris in Zones 4-8. The crested, slender and vernal irises do best in a moist, acid soil, pH 5.0 to 6.5, enriched with peat moss or compost. The dwarf bearded iris does best in a neutral soil, pH 7.0. All four species grow well in the high, open shade of deciduous trees, but the dwarf bearded iris is also recommended for full sun. Plant irises in the spring or fall, spacing smaller-growing species 6 to 9 inches apart, larger-growing species 12 to 18 inches apart. Prepare soil by digging a hole and mounding soil into it. Place the rhizome on top of the mound and spread out the thin, fibrous roots over the top. To prevent rotting, rhizomes of crested and dwarf bearded iris should only be half buried, with tips facing out from the center. Keep the soil moist around the rhizomes for several weeks. Irises are most often propagated by dividing the rhizomes, making sure each division has one, and preferably two, growth buds. Divide the slender iris in early spring before flowering; all other species should be divided after flowering.

J

JACK-IN-THE-PULPIT See *Arisaema*
JAPANESE HOLLY See *Ilex*
JASMINE, PINE ROCK See *Androsace*
JASMINE, ROCK See *Androsace*

JEFFERSONIA

J. diphylla (American twinleaf); *J. dubia* (Manchurian twinleaf)

These perennial spring-blooming woodland wildflowers are best grown in large clumps in a shady rock garden, although they may also be grown in pots in a cool alpine greenhouse. Jeffersonias spread by means of moplike clumps of rootlets. Their anemone-like flowers, up to 1½ inches across, are white or pale lavender-blue and are borne singly atop leafless stems. The winglike leaf, so deeply divided that it appears to be two leaves instead of one, wraps around the stem of the flower, slowly unfolding as the flower fades. The flower stem continues to grow, sometimes tripling its original height, and in late summer produces a pear-shaped seed pod.

American twinleaf grows 6 to 8 inches high, with an 8- to 10-inch flower stem that continues to elongate to about 18

AMERICAN TWINLEAF
Jeffersonia diphylla

inches. Its white flowers are 1 inch wide, its twin leaves 4 inches wide. Manchurian twinleaf has lavender-blue flowers 1¼ inches wide. It grows 4 to 6 inches tall and its flower stalk may grow 12 inches tall. Its less-divided twin leaves are 3 inches across and when young are copper-purple.

HOW TO GROW. Jeffersonias are hardy in Zones 4-8 and do best in the open shade of a deciduous woodland. They need a moist, sandy soil enriched with peat moss or leaf mold, with a pH of 5.5 to 7.0. Set out plants in early spring or fall, spacing them 6 to 8 inches apart. In climates where there is intermittent snowfall, mulch with leaves in the fall. Propagate additional plants from seeds sown as soon as they ripen and held over the winter in a cold frame; it will be three years, however, before seed-grown plants flower. Established plants seed themselves.

JULIA PRIMROSE See *Primula*
JUNGFRAU SAXIFRAGE See *Saxifraga*
JUNIPER THRIFT See *Armeria*

K

KEW BROOM See *Cytisus*
KINGSVILLE DWARF BOXWOOD See *Buxus*
KINNIKINNICK See *Arctostaphylos*

L

LARCHLEAF SANDWORT See *Arenaria*
LEADWORT See *Ceratostigma*
LEEK, LILY See *Allium*

LEONTOPODIUM
L. alpinum (edelweiss)

This famous but modest flower readily makes its home in the crevices of a wall garden or a stony moraine. Covered with woolly white hairs, edelweiss forms bushy mounds about 8 inches high and 9 inches wide. The narrow gray-green leaves grow mainly near the base of the stem, which bears star-shaped flowers in the summer. The flowers are made up of tight clusters of round yellow heads, ¼ inch in diameter, surrounded by five to 15 velvety white petal-like bracts ½ to 1 inch long. These star-shaped bracts adorn the caps of European mountain climbers. The roots of edelweiss are far-ranging but short-lived; though a perennial, the plant normally does not survive more than two or three years. The variety Stracheyi grows taller, has larger flowers and lives longer—about four years—and Soulei is a dwarf variety that lives indefinitely if divided every second spring.

HOW TO GROW. Edelweiss is hardy in Zones 4-8. It requires a sunny location and a light, well-drained, sandy soil with pH of 6.5 to 7.5. Sand, gravel or gritty lime should be worked into the soil to lighten it, as edelweiss cannot stand much moisture. Seeds may not ripen in wet summers, and roots rot in wet winters. Plant edelweiss in spring, setting the plants 6 inches apart. Propagate from seed, sown as soon as it ripens or early in the spring, or divide the roots in early spring. Plants started from seed flower the second year.

LEWISIA
L. cotyledon (Siskiyou lewisia); *L. rediviva* (bitter-root); *L. tweedyi* (tweedy lewisia)

In mountains of the West, lewisias can be found growing in the crevices of bare rock, making them ideal for an alpine scree or the crevices of rock walls and paving stones. Growing from carrot-like taproots, they spread by forming rosettes on these roots; each new rosette develops its own fleshy root. Lewisias bloom from late spring through summer.

For climate zones and frost dates, see maps, pages 150-151.

EDELWEISS
Leontopodium alpinum

BITTER-ROOT
Lewisia rediviva

Siskiyou lewisia has evergreen tongue-shaped leaves, 3 inches long, sometimes with wavy edges. It forms rosettes 6 inches wide, and its flowers bloom in clusters on stems 4 to 12 inches high. Each flower, up to 1½ inches wide, is white flushed or veined with red. There are also pink, clear white and yellow varieties. Tweedy lewisia, another evergreen, bears one to three apricot-pink flowers, about 2½ inches wide, on 6-inch stems. A single plant may produce more than 50 flowers during its blooming season. The broad, light-green leaves, often tinged with red, form rosettes 9 inches wide.

Bitter-root, a deciduous plant, produces clumps of narrow, stemless, succulent leaves, 1 to 4 inches long, in the fall. This foliage lasts through the winter and into the following summer, when the almost stemless flowers appear. These are pink or white, 1 to 2 inches across. As the flowers fade, the plant becomes dormant, disappearing until autumn when new leaves emerge.

HOW TO GROW. These three lewisias are hardy in Zones 2-7. Siskiyou lewisia and tweedy lewisia grow best in partial shade, bitter-root in full sun. They all need a deep, well-drained sandy soil with an acid pH of 5.5 to 6.5. A mixture of 1 part fine stone chips, 1 part sand and 1 part acid leaf mold is recommended. Give Siskiyou lewisia a cool location, such as a north slope or wall.

Plant lewisias in the spring, setting the root crown about an inch above the soil, so moisture will drain away from the crown, minimizing the danger of rot; crown rot will cause the plant to die after flowering. Siskiyou and tweedy lewisias need to have some moisture during the spring and summer, but wetness in winter will kill them; bitter-root in contrast requires dry soil and intense heat during the summer, when it is in its period of dormancy.

Propagate all lewisias from seed sown in the fall or by cutting off rosettes in spring and rooting them in sand. Plants started from seed require several months of cold weather to germinate. Therefore, sow seeds outdoors in autumn, barely covering them with sandy soil, or refrigerate them over winter and sow in spring. Transplant the seedlings to individual containers and keep them in a cold frame for one or two full seasons before setting them in the garden. Plants grown from seed flower in three years.

LILY LEEK See *Allium*
LIVERLEAF See *Hepatica*
LOW POPPY MALLOW See *Callirhoe*

M

MAHOGANY FAWN LILY See *Erythronium*
MANCHURIAN TWINLEAF See *Jeffersonia*
MISSOURI PRIMROSE See *Oenothera*

MITCHELLA

M. repens (partridgeberry, checkerberry, squawberry)

A woodland wildflower of eastern North America, partridgeberry is used to carpet shaded areas of rock gardens or to ramble along the stone of a footpath. An evergreen perennial, its thin trailing stems, up to 15 inches long, are lined with pairs of dark green glossy round leaves, ¾ inch wide. Often the leaves have white veins. In summer, it bears fragrant white or pale pink trumpet-shaped flowers, ½ inch long, in pairs on 2-inch stalks. Each of these is followed by a fused brilliant-red berry, ¼ inch in diameter, which decorates the evergreen plant all winter. Partridgeberry spreads by branching stems, which take root at the joints.

HOW TO GROW. Partridgeberry is hardy in Zones 3-8 and is suited to northern gardens. It needs shade or partial shade

PARTRIDGEBERRY

Mitchella repens

and a cool, moist climate. A rich, gritty, acid soil with a pH of 4.5 to 6.0 is ideal. Propagate from seeds sown in the spring or by dividing rooted stems, also in the spring.

MOSS PHLOX See *Phlox*
MOSS PINK See *Phlox*
MOSS SANDWORT See *Arenaria*
MOUNTAIN ALYSSUM See *Alyssum*
MOUNTAIN AVENS See *Dryas*
MOUNTAIN BUTTERCUP See *Ranunculus*
MOUNTAIN ROCK CRESS See *Arabis*
MOUNTAIN SANDWORT See *Arenaria*
MOUSE-EAR GYPSOPHILA See *Gypsophila*

MUSCARI
M. botryoides (common grape hyacinth); *M. latifolium; M. tubergenianum,* also called *M. aucheri tubergenianum* (Tubergen grape hyacinth)

Among the heralds of spring, grape hyacinths are ideally suited for massed plantings in sunny rock gardens and alpine meadows. These tiny bulb plants form clumps of grasslike leaves 6 to 12 inches tall; they push up through the soil in fall, last through the winter, then die down to the ground by summer. Their fragrant urn-shaped flowers, each less than ¼ inch wide, appear in grapelike clusters on 6- to 9-inch flower spikes in spring.

Common grape hyacinth produces blue flowers with white tips but has a variety, Album, with white flowers. *M. latifolium* bears dark purple flowers, and Tubergen grape hyacinth has flowers that shade from light blue at the bottom of the spike to dark blue at the top. All grape hyacinths spread moderately fast by developing little bulbs around the larger ones and by seeding themselves. These hardy perennials can even grow through the dense root system of thick grass.

HOW TO GROW. Grape hyacinths are hardy in Zones 2-10. They do best in full sun but will tolerate partial shade; in deep shade, plants produce more leaves than flowers. They thrive in moist, rich, well-drained soil with a pH of 5.5 to 7.0. Set bulbs in the ground as soon as they are available, in late summer or early fall. Place them 2 to 3 inches deep and 3 to 4 inches apart. Keep moist during the growing season. These bulbs do not need any winter protection or fertilizer, and may be left in the ground indefinitely. Divide plants in midsummer, when they are dormant. Propagate by separating the small bulb clumps every three years.

O

OCTOBER DAPHNE See *Sedum*
OCTOBER PLANT See *Sedum*

OENOTHERA
O. missourensis (Ozark sundrops, Missouri primrose)

Ozark sundrops, prairie natives, fit well in a rocky meadow setting, and stage a splendid show in wall pockets or on the surface of scree. They have dark trailing stems, up to 15 inches long, which turn upright to form broad mounds, 6 to 12 inches high. The narrow oval leaves, 3 to 5 inches long, are covered with silvery hairs, and from summer to late fall, satiny trumpet-shaped yellow flowers, up to 5 inches wide, provide a spectacular display. They open late in the day, stay open until dawn and are faintly fragrant. The flowers are followed by 2- to 3-inch-long seed pods. Ozark sundrops are perennials, but die back to the ground in winter. They will live 20 years or more.

HOW TO GROW. Ozark sundrops are hardy in Zones 4-8 and grow best in a dry, sandy or gravelly lime-enriched soil with

COMMON GRAPE HYACINTH
Muscari botryoides

OZARK SUNDROPS
Oenothera missourensis

For climate zones and frost dates, see maps, pages 150-151.

BLUE-EYED MARY
Omphalodes verna

MOSS PINK
Phlox subulata

an alkaline pH of 7.0 to 8.0. Good drainage is important, for the plant is susceptible to rot. Set out plants in the garden in spring, spacing them 12 to 15 inches apart. Propagate Ozark sundrops from seeds sown outdoors as soon as they ripen, or start seeds in late winter in a cold frame or greenhouse. Alternatively, root stem cuttings taken in summer.

OLYMPIC ST.-JOHN'S-WORT See *Hypericum*

OMPHALODES
O. verna (blue-eyed Mary)

Blue-eyed Mary, reputed to be the favorite flower of Marie Antoinette, is a creeping perennial for woodland rock gardens. It spreads rapidly on horizontal, jointed stems to form 4- to 5-inch-high mats of dark green, heart-shaped leaves, 1 to 4 inches long. In spring, ½-inch-wide bright blue flowers with white throats bloom in pairs on erect flower stalks that rise above the foliage. The flowers are followed by seed pods that split into four segments when ripe. The foliage of blue-eyed Mary is evergreen in the South, but elsewhere it dies down in the winter.

HOW TO GROW. Blue-eyed Mary is hardy in Zones 5-8. It thrives in almost any degree of shade and grows best in moist sandy or gritty soil with a pH of 6.0 to 7.5. Sow seeds in the spring where they are to grow, thinning the seedlings to stand 8 inches apart. Once established, blue-eyed Mary requires little care. Propagate from seed or by dividing rooted stems in the spring or fall.

OZARK SUNDROPS See *Oenothera*

P

PACIFIC BLEEDING HEART See *Dicentra*
PARTRIDGEBERRY See *Mitchella*
PASQUE FLOWER, SPREADING See *Anemone*

PHLOX
P. bifida (sand phlox); *P. stolonifera* (creeping phlox); *P. subulata* (moss pink, ground pink, moss phlox)

Phlox, a native American perennial, includes these three low-growing species that are suitable for carpeting rock walls and banks with sheets of lavish spring color. On most of them the flowers bloom in loose clusters of four to 10 flowers. Sand phlox is a midwestern species that forms cushions up to 10 inches tall. It has narrow light-green leaves, up to 1½ inches long, and woody, tangled stems. The 1-inch flowers, ranging from white to pale violet, have deeply notched petals. Sand phlox sends down a long, thick taproot, and fast drainage is required to prevent the taproot from rotting.

Creeping phlox is an eastern woodland species. It spreads rapidly on stems that root wherever nodes touch the ground, forming broad mats of foliage. Creeping phlox, which grows 6 to 12 inches high, is commonly used as a ground cover. Its broad oval leaves, about 1½ inches across, are covered with downy hairs and lie flat on the ground, forming a dense carpet. The flowers, 1 inch across, are usually blue or purple but may occasionally be pink or white.

Moss pink, an eastern species, also stays green year-round in mild climates. It forms dense mats of foliage, 6 inches high, by sending out rooting stems and is often used as a ground cover. Tiny needle-like leaves cover its stems, and it flowers profusely. The many varieties of moss pink offer a wide choice of flowers with round, narrow, notched or star-like petals, in a range of colors that includes white, lilac, lavender, pink, rose, magenta and blue. In many varieties, the flowers are fragrant.

HOW TO GROW. These three species of phlox are hardy in Zones 3-8. Sand phlox needs full sun and a well-drained, sandy soil with a pH of 6.0 to 7.5. Creeping phlox grows best in shade or dappled sunlight in soil enriched with leaf mold, pH 5.5 to 7.0. Moss pink, the easiest species to grow, thrives in full sun in almost any well-drained soil. Phlox may be grown from seed, sown in spring or fall, or from nursery plants set out in the spring or autumn and spaced about 10 inches apart. To stimulate fresh growth and sometimes renew blooming, shear the foliage after flowering.

Propagation of the various phloxes depends on their root structure and growing habits. Established clumps of creeping phlox and moss pink may be divided in the spring after flowering. New plants of these species may also be started from seed—both seed themselves freely. Or they may be started from tip cuttings taken in summer, to flower the following year. Sand phlox cannot be divided because of its deep taproot; it is not easy to transplant. To propagate sand phlox, cover the crown of the plant with sand; roots will grow along the stems, which can then be cut off and moved.

PICEA

P. abies 'Little Gem' (small bird's-nest spruce); *P. abies* 'Pygmaea' (pygmy Norway spruce); *P. abies* 'Repens'; *P. glauca* 'Conica' (dwarf Alberta spruce); *P. mariana* 'Nana' (dwarf black spruce)

Useful as small evergreen accent shrubs in a rock garden, the dwarf spruces, like their full-sized counterparts, are notable for their tolerance of high winds and low temperatures. They may grow as rounded globes or as spreading plants, much wider than they are high. The sharp, stiff needles are usually dark green. The fast-growing fibrous root system is wide and deep, adapting to a wide variety of locations.

Little Gem is a very small mutation of Nidiformis, one of the dwarf Norway spruces, and like Nidiformis it is spreading in habit, with a flattened top that has a slight bird's-nest depression in the center. Little Gem is a very formal, tidy plant with tiny dark green needles; it develops very slowly and never becomes more than 1 to 2 feet high and 2 to 3 feet wide.

The pygmy Norway spruce forms a dense bush of uneven shape that ultimately reaches 12 inches tall and 20 inches across. The shape may vary from broadly conical to rounded to urn-shaped. Growth each year varies from ½ inch to 4 inches. The small, thick needles are pale green when young, turning darker with age.

P. abies Repens grows horizontally over the ground on slender, arching branches that build up in layers to form a dense, uniform silhouette. The needles, growing in flattened sprays, are pale green when they are young and darken with age. A plant may reach 12 to 24 inches in height and have a spread of 5 feet, but its growth is slow and it may not reach this size for 25 years.

The dwarf Alberta spruce is a compact conical tree with dense dark green foliage. It grows slowly, reaching a height of 10 feet in 40 years, and is seldom more than 4 feet wide. The dwarf black spruce Nana forms a dense, rounded shrub 12 inches high and 24 inches wide. The branches subdivide into smaller and smaller offshoots, all covered with flattened green needles.

HOW TO GROW. These dwarf spruces grow well in Zones 2-7 and respond best to full sun, although partial shade is tolerated. Ideally, they should have a moist, well-drained soil enriched with peat moss or leaf mold and having a slightly acid pH of 5.5 to 6.5., but they will survive in dry soil. Plant these spruces in early spring or autumn. Mulch young plants

DWARF ALBERTA SPRUCE
Picea glauca 'Conica'

For climate zones and frost dates, see maps, pages 150-151.

THREE-TOOTHED CINQUEFOIL
Potentilla tridentata

AURICULA PRIMROSE
Primula auricula

with peat moss, compost or shredded leaves, and water them thoroughly during periods of drought.

PINK, GROUND or MOSS See *Phlox*
POLYANTHUS PRIMROSE See *Primula*

POTENTILLA

P. alba (white cinquefoil); *P. tridentata* (three-toothed cinquefoil, wineleaf cinquefoil)

Mixed with heathers in an alpine garden, where growing conditions approximate the rocky outcrops of high mountains, these two low-growing cinquefoils offer small size, hardiness and interesting foliage. The name cinquefoil refers to their finger-like leaflets, which typically occur in groups of five, although there are also three- and seven-fingered forms. Flowers, too, are five petaled, and tend to be saucer shaped like the flowers of a wild rose.

The white cinquefoil forms low, spreading mounds 5 to 8 inches high. Its five-part leaves are smooth and green on the upper side but are covered with silky white hairs beneath, giving the foliage a glistening appearance. Sprays of white 1-inch flowers bloom on 6-inch stems throughout most of the summer. The three-toothed cinquefoil grows 6 to 12 inches high and is open enough for bulbs to grow beneath it. It bears sprays of ¼-inch-wide white flowers, resembling strawberry blossoms, but its chief ornament is its foliage. The shiny dark green leaves are made up of three ½- to 1-inch leaflets, each tipped at the end with three teeth. The three-toothed cinquefoil is evergreen in the warmer part of its range but in cooler regions turns brilliant red in the fall. Both of these species spread by means of creeping underground stems, the white cinquefoil spreading more slowly than three-toothed cinquefoil.

HOW TO GROW. Three-toothed cinquefoil is hardy in Zones 2-8, white cinquefoil in Zones 4-8. Both require full sun and thrive in a well-drained garden soil, though the foliage of three-toothed cinquefoil will color more deeply if the soil is acid, pH 5.0 to 6.0. Neither species requires much water. Set out plants in the spring, spacing them 10 inches apart. Once established, cinquefoils require little care except pruning to remove deadwood and the unsightly seed pods of the three-toothed cinquefoil. Propagate by dividing roots in spring or fall or from cuttings of ripe shoots taken in the fall. New plants may also be started from seed in the spring.

PRIMROSE See *Primula*
PRIMROSE, MISSOURI See *Oenothera*

PRIMULA

P. auricula (auricula primrose); *P. denticulata* (Himalayan primrose); *P. juliae* (Julia primrose); *P. polyantha* (polyanthus primrose); *P. sieboldii* (Siebold's primrose); *P. veris,* also called *P. officinalis* (cowslip); *P. vulgaris,* also called *P. acaulis* (English primrose)

Treasured for their brilliant spring flowers, primroses play many roles in the rock garden. With more than 500 kinds to choose from, some rock gardeners use nothing else. Most are suited to moist, partially shaded environments; some even grow in bogs. Others, the more succulent types, need good drainage and bright light, like that on alpine moraines. The following are recommended for color and ease of growth.

Auricula primrose is an alpine species suitable for use in a moraine, raised bed or rock wall. Its thick, oval, powdery gray-green leaves form rosettes 6 inches high that last the year around. The species bears fragrant clear yellow flowers in midspring. Hybrids come in almost every color, usually with contrasting centers. One of the hybrids is *P. pubescens*, which needs similar growing conditions. It forms 8-inch-high rosettes of gray-green leaves and bears rose-crimson flowers with white centers. Himalayan primrose, also with powdery foliage, is a 4- to 6-inch-tall plant that produces many sturdy flower stalks, 8 to 12 inches tall, bearing 2-inch globes of mauve flowers in moist soil.

Julia primrose is a dwarf species only 3 inches high. Its creeping stems bear tufts of heart-shaped leaves and 1-inch-wide reddish-purple flowers with yellow eyes. The flowers, on 2-inch stalks, are so thick they hide the foliage. More common are its hybrids, called the Juliana primroses, which come in many colors. Polyanthus primroses are evergreen hybrids that form clumps of rosettes up to 1 foot tall. Their flower stalks bear clusters of single or double flowers up to 1½ inches wide in a broad range of colors that includes pastels as well as striped and blended forms.

Siebold's primrose, a Japanese species, is 6 to 8 inches high and has toothed leaves 3 to 4 inches long that die down in late summer and reappear the following spring. The flowers are 2 inches wide, with white, pink or purple petals and colored centers. Cowslip is about 8 inches tall. It blooms in midspring, normally bearing tubular cream to yellow flowers, though copper, red, purple and double yellow forms are also available. English primrose, a hardy perennial 6 inches high, bears fragrant 1-inch yellow flowers that bloom singly rather than in clusters. It comes in many varieties, in other colors, with larger flowers and different shapes.

HOW TO GROW. Auricula and polyanthus primroses and cowslips are hardy in Zones 3-8; Himalayan, Julia, Siebold's and English primroses in Zones 4-8. A cool, moist climate in summer suits primroses best. Auricula primrose requires well-drained neutral soil, pH 6.0 to 7.5, and moderate sun. Plant these species so moisture will drain away from the crowns; otherwise they will rot. Other species require an acid soil, pH 5.5 to 6.5, enriched with leaf mold or compost, and grow best in the partial shade of deciduous trees. Himalayan primrose thrives in bog or woodland conditions, and Siebold's primrose adapts to deep shade or moderate sun as well as light shade.

Set out plants in spring, spacing them 6 to 12 inches apart. Keep the soil moist during the growing season, and mulch in winter with a light covering of straw or salt hay. Feed annually in the spring with a balanced fertilizer, such as 10-10-10. Dig up and divide crowded clumps at once after flowering.

Primroses, which spread by forming side rosettes, can be propagated by rooting these offsets after flowering. Many species seed themselves, but the seedlings may not breed true to form, and are often not worth keeping.

PROSTRATE BROOM See *Cytisus*
PURPLE ROCK CRESS See *Aubrieta*
PYGMY NORWAY SPRUCE See *Picea*

R

RANUNCULUS
R. montanus, also called *R. geraniifolius* (mountain buttercup)

A charming dwarf species of the familiar field flower, mountain buttercups are alpine plants, suitable for growing in gardens that simulate rocky outcrops and scree conditions. They form 6-inch-high mats of dense, dark green foliage, the lower leaves being nearly round while the upper ones are divided into 3 to 5 parts. In spring, shiny-petaled bright yellow flowers, 1 inch wide, bloom on 6-inch stems, followed by tiny clusters of dry fruits containing the buttercup seeds.

For climate zones and frost dates, see maps, pages 150-151.

HIMALAYAN PRIMROSE
Primula denticulata

COWSLIP
Primula veris

MOUNTAIN BUTTERCUP
Ranunculus montanus

DWARF RHODODENDRON
Rhododendron 'Dora Amateis'

The mountain buttercup is a perennial that spreads slowly by underground stems called stolons.

HOW TO GROW. Mountain buttercups are hardy in Zones 3-7. They grow in either partial shade or full sun and adapt to any ordinary garden soil but grow best in a moist, well-drained, gritty, acid loam with a pH of 5.0 to 6.5, enriched with leaf mold or compost. Water during dry spells, as the roots are close to the surface. Mountain buttercup seeds, unless very fresh, may not germinate. It is better to propagate plants by dividing the stolons after flowering.

RHODODENDRON

R. fastigiatum; R. indicum 'Balsaminiflorum' (Balsam azalea); *R. indicum* 'Flame Creeper'; *R. keiskei* 'Dwarf' (dwarf Keisk rhododendron); *R. kiusianum* (dwarf azalea); *R. nakaharai* (dwarf azalea); *R. racemosum* 'Dwarf' (dwarf Mayflower rhododendron); *R.* hybrids 'Dora Amateis,' 'Moerheim,' 'Purple Gem' (all called dwarf rhododendron or dwarf azalea)

The enormous rhododendron family, which includes both rhododendrons and azaleas, contains many dwarf plants suitable for rock gardens, their specific use depending on their soil and light preferences and their habits of growth—compact, spreading or trailing. All the species and varieties listed here are evergreen and notable either for their foliage or flowers, sometimes for both. Most have oval leaves, dull or shiny; their flowers, bell-shaped or trumpet-shaped, usually bloom in clusters from early spring to early summer.

R. fastigiatum, a dwarf rhododendron, has shiny blue-gray leaves, ½ inch long, and bell-shaped lavender-rose flowers 1 inch wide. It is an open, upright plant, becoming 3 feet tall with a spread of 12 to 24 inches. The Balsam and Flame Creeper azaleas are prostrate plants that form low mounds up to 4 feet across; they are useful as ground covers. Both have dull, hairy leaves, 2 inches long. The salmon-pink double flowers of Balsam resemble roses, while those of Flame Creeper are an intense scarlet. The dwarf Keisk rhododendron bears pale yellow 2-inch bell-shaped flowers and has olive-green 2-inch leaves that turn wine red in winter. It is a spreading plant, growing 2½ feet tall and 4 feet wide.

R. kiusianum and *R. nakaharai* are both dwarf azaleas. *R. kiusianum* blooms while still young, bearing white, pink, rose or purple flowers 1 to 1½ inches across. The shiny 1-inch leaves sometimes turn red in winter. This open, twiggy plant grows slowly to 3 feet tall and 5 feet wide. *R. nakaharai* forms a low dense mound that seems to grow flatter as it matures, since its ultimate height is 6 to 9 inches, while its spread is 12 to 15 inches. The small, shiny leaves, 2 inches long, are hairy on the undersides. The 3-inch pink, salmon or red flowers are saucer shaped and, unlike most azaleas, open in midsummer. The dwarf Mayflower rhododendron is a spreading semiprostrate plant 2 feet high and up to 5 feet wide, with many-branched wiry stems. The ¾-inch white or pink flowers begin to appear while the plant is still quite young. The 2-inch leaves are smooth on the top, gray and scaly on the underside.

Dora Amateis, Moerheim and Purple Gem are all dwarf rhododendrons. Dora Amateis grows 3 to 4 feet tall and has 3-inch white flowers speckled with green; its leaves are dark green and in full sun have a bronze sheen. Moerheim is a low, dense shrub, growing 3 feet high and 3 feet wide; it has 1-inch violet-to-purple flowers, and 2-inch shiny green leaves that turn maroon in the winter. Purple Gem forms a dense mound and grows 1½ to 2 feet tall; this variety has 2-inch lavender-to-purple flowers and 2-inch blue-green leaves that turn rust-colored as they age.

HOW TO GROW. All dwarf rhododendrons and azaleas are hardy in Zones 6-10, and many can be grown, if given protection, in Zone 5. In cold climates, most do better on the north side of a building or on a northwest slope. All need some sun for best flowering but in general require partial shade. They thrive in a moist, well-drained, humus-filled soil with a pH of 5.0 to 6.0, enriched with peat moss or leaf mold. Plant dwarf rhododendrons and azaleas in spring or, in areas that have mild winters, in the fall. Prepare the soil by thoroughly mixing equal parts of loam, coarse sand and ground oak leaves or redwood. Plant the root ball slightly higher than it was growing at the nursery.

To keep the soil cool and moist, mulch it with a 2-inch layer of wood chips, ground bark, pine needles or coarse peat moss. Fertilize plants in the early spring with a light sprinkling of cottonseed meal or a fertilizer specially formulated for acid-loving plants. Pruning is seldom needed except for removal of faded flowers, but if it is, branches may be trimmed immediately after flowering. Rhododendrons may be harmed in winter by drying winds and bright sun; protect their shallow roots with a mulch of oak leaves or pine needles and their foliage with a loose blanket of evergreen boughs or specially built screens.

ROCK COLUMBINE, ALPINE See *Aquilegia*
ROCK JASMINE, PINE See *Androsace*
ROCK SOAPWORT See *Saponaria*
ROSE DAPHNE See *Daphne*
ROUGH GENTIAN See *Gentiana*
RUE ANEMONE See *Anemonella*

S

SAFFRON CROCUS See *Crocus*
ST.-JOHN'S-WORT See *Hypericum*
SAND PHLOX See *Phlox*
SANDWORT See *Arenaria*

SAPONARIA
S. ocymoides (rock soapwort)

In summer, European railway embankments are bright with the flowers of this alpine plant, rock soapwort. In a rock garden it provides a similar blanket of color for boulders, rocky outcrops and dry stone walls. Rock soapwort spreads by means of underground rhizomes, from which it sends up many-branched stems covered with soft, thick leaves, ½ to 1 inch long, downy above and usually red-tinged beneath. The ½-inch flowers, borne in loose clusters, have bright pink petals, deeper pink tubular bases and purple throats; there is also a pure white variety. This vigorous plant spreads several feet in a few years to form a mat 6 to 12 inches high, and may need to be cut back to keep it within bounds.

HOW TO GROW. Rock soapwort is hardy in Zones 2-8 and is exceptionally easy to grow. It does well in any open, sunny situation and in ordinary garden soil, though a light, gritty alpine soil with a pH of 6.0 to 7.5 suits it best; it does not need much moisture. Sow seeds or set out nursery plants in the spring or autumn, setting them about 12 inches apart. After the plants have flowered, cut the largest stems back almost to the ground to keep the plants neat and compact. Rock soapwort seeds itself freely and takes care of its propagation without human help, but additional plants may also be started from stem cuttings, taken in the summer, or by dividing the rhizomes in early spring.

SAVORYLEAF ASTER See *Aster*
SAWARA FALSE CYPRESS See *Chamaecyparis*

For climate zones and frost dates, see maps, pages 150-151.

DWARF KEISK RHODODENDRON
Rhododendron keiskei 'Dwarf'

ROCK SOAPWORT
Saponaria ocymoides

JUNGFRAU SAXIFRAGE
Saxifraga cotyledon

SAXIFRAGE
Saxifraga kabschia 'Ferdinandi-Coburgi'

SAXIFRAGA

S. cochlearis (snail saxifrage); *S. cotyledon* (jungfrau saxifrage); *S. kabschia* 'Ferdinandi-Coburgi'; *S. marginata* (horn-rim saxifrage); *S. paniculata*, also called *S. aizoon* (aizoon saxifrage); *S. stolonifera*, also called *S. sarmentosa* (strawberry saxifrage)

The saxifrages are alpine plants par excellence; there are more than 300 different species growing in the crevices of rocks all over the world. In fact, the Latin word *saxifraga* means rock breaker. Most of them are low-growing perennials that spread on creeping stems, sending up rosettes or clumps of foliage to form thick mats. Often the leaves are thick and fleshy, and many of them are edged with silvery deposits of lime that make them appear translucent. The flowers are usually star shaped and in many species are borne in loose sprays on tall stalks that rise above the foliage.

The snail saxifrage has lime-encrusted 1-inch-long spoon-shaped leaves with toothed margins. They form rosettes of foliage 2 to 3 inches high and 9 to 12 inches wide. The white flowers, up to ¾ inch across, bloom in the late spring on 18-inch reddish stalks. Jungfrau saxifrage forms 4-inch-wide pyramid-shaped rosettes of tongue-shaped leaves with lime-beaded edges. The branched flower stalks rise like plumes as much as 3 feet high, bearing ¾-inch white flowers that may be speckled with red or purple spots; they bloom in early summer. The hybrid saxifrage Ferdinandi-Coburgi forms rosettes of gray-green lime-encrusted leaves, ½ inch long, that create small, dense hummocks 6 to 8 inches across. The ½-inch saucer-shaped flowers are yellow and rise on 3-inch stalks. Hornrim saxifrage grows in 3-inch-high tufts of blunt-tipped lime-encrusted leaves, ½ inch long. Its 3-inch flower stalks bear white or pale pink flowers, ½ inch wide, in late spring and summer.

Aizoon saxifrage forms dense 6-inch-wide rosettes of narrow spoon-shaped leaves, 1½ inches long, with toothed and lime-encrusted margins. The ½-inch-wide flowers are cream-white with purple dots and bloom in summer. The many varieties of aizoon saxifrage offer different flower colors and leaf forms. Strawberry saxifrage forms tufts of foliage 4 to 5 inches high and spreads on thin, threadlike runners, similar to those of the strawberry plant, extending out from the base of the plant as much as several feet. The 3-inch-wide leaves are round, green on top and red beneath, with silvery veins. In summer, sprays of white flowers 1 to 1½ inches wide bloom on 6- to 8-inch stalks.

HOW TO GROW. The saxifrages are hardy in Zones 3-6, and grow best in partial shade or dappled sunlight. They thrive among rocks in a well-drained gritty soil with a pH of 6.5 to 7.5. Set out plants in early spring or early fall, spacing them 6 inches apart. Or start plants from seed sown thinly in early spring on top of a fine layer of gravel spread over gritty fertile soil. Transplant seedlings in about a year, when they are large enough to handle. Propagate by separating offsets after flowering, treating them as cuttings. To stimulate the growth of new rosettes on old plants, spread a thin layer of sifted loam, leaf mold and sand over the top of the plants.

SAXIFRAGE See *Saxifraga*
SCHAFTA CAMPION See *Silene*
SCOTCH HEATHER See *Calluna*
SEA PINK See *Armeria*

SEDUM

S. cauticola; S. ewersii (Ewers stonecrop); *S. rupestre; S. sieboldii* (October plant, October daphne, Siebold stonecrop); *S. spathulifolium; S. spurium* (two-row stonecrop)

The sedums are creeping succulents that are very easy to grow and are ideal for draping rock walls and carpeting poor, dry soil. These six species also bear outstanding flowers. The foliage is usually evergreen or semievergreen, depending on the severity of winter cold, and often turns purple in autumn. All are perennials spreading on rooting stems. *S. cauticola*, 3 inches high, has 8-inch stems laden with pairs of roundish blue-green leaves with red edges. Rose-red flowers ½ inch across bloom in flat clusters up to 4 inches wide in late summer and early fall. Ewers stonecrop, 6 to 12 inches high, has stems 6 to 12 inches long, which appear to pass through the centers of roundish blue-gray leaves about ¾ inch wide. Its pink or pale violet flowers bloom in late summer in rounded clusters 2 inches across.

S. *rupestre* is 8 to 12 inches high; its narrow ½-inch-long blue-green leaves grow thickly along its 10-inch stems. It blooms in late spring and early summer in flattened 2-inch clusters of golden yellow flowers. October plant, up to 12 inches high, has arching, purple-tinged stems bearing whorls of three round leaves 1 inch across with wavy pink edges. Flat clusters of small pink flowers bloom in fall. The entire plant dies down in winter. S. *spathulifolium*, 3 to 6 inches high, has rosettes of 1-inch-long blue-green leaves that are often tinged with red. The ⅝-inch yellow flowers bloom in flat clusters 2 to 3 inches wide in late spring. Two-row stonecrop, 9 inches high, has oval leaves 1 inch long with wavy edges. Its flowers are white, pink or red, up to ½ inch across, and bloom in summer in flat 2- to 3-inch clusters.

HOW TO GROW. October plant is hardy in Zones 4-8, S. *spathulifolium* in Zones 5-8. S. *cauticola*, Ewers stonecrop, and two-row stonecrop are hardy in Zones 4-10. Sedums grow well in full sun or light shade. Plant S. *spathulifolium* in light, moist humus; the other sedums will tolerate almost any well-drained soil and even periods of drought. They spread rampantly in fertile soil, slowly in poor soil. Set out plants at any time during the growing season. Sedums do not need fertilizing. Propagate sedums by dividing plants or from stem cuttings, which are quick to root.

SEMPERVIVUM

S. *arachnoideum* (cobweb houseleek, spiderweb houseleek); S. *tectorum* (common houseleek, hen-and-chickens); S. hybrids.

The houseleeks are alpine perennials that grow with only a trace of soil, covering rocks and dry walls in almost any well-drained situation. Their succulent-leaved rosettes multiply almost as you watch; the mother plant is soon surrounded by numerous offshoots, giving rise to a popular name, hen-and-chickens. Houseleeks bloom in the summer, but their main attraction is the color, texture and pattern of their foliage. After flowering, the mother rosette usually dies, but the offsets continue to spread. A single rosette may form a yard-wide colony of several hundred houseleeks in only a few years. There are about 20 species and several hundred hybrids and cultivated varieties.

Cobweb houseleek forms a ¼- to ¾-inch ball of some 50 pointed leaves draped with cobweb-like strands of white hair. The outer leaves are tinged with red. The flowers are rose-colored and bloom in sprays of 9 to 12 flowers, about 1 inch wide, on a 3- to 4-inch-high stalk. The common houseleek forms 3- to 4-inch-wide flattened rosettes of wedge-shaped leaves ending in a sharp point; they are pale green tipped with purple. The 9-inch-tall hairy flower stalks bear sprays of star-shaped rose-colored flowers 1 inch wide. Common houseleek is one of the fastest spreading species. In Europe, it is often planted on thatched roofs for insulation

For climate zones and frost dates, see maps, pages 150-151.

Sedum rupestre

OCTOBER PLANT
Sedum sieboldii

COMMON HOUSELEEK
Sempervivum tectorum

SCHAFTA CAMPION
Silene schafta

and to protect the thatch from fire. The many hybrid forms of sempervivum offer a wide range of leaf shapes, sizes and colors, including bronze-green, silver, pale green-tinted violet and jade green.

HOW TO GROW. Houseleeks are hardy in Zones 3-10 except on the Gulf Coast. They grow well in full sun, but the rosettes will be larger and more open in partial shade. Almost any well-drained soil with a pH of 5.5 to 7.5 suits them, so long as it is not too wet. Plant them in fall or spring, spacing them 6 to 9 inches apart; they will quickly fill in the gaps. Do not fertilize houseleeks. Propagate additional plants by separating offsets at any time.

SIEBOLD STONECROP See *Sedum*
SIEBOLD'S PRIMROSE See *Primula*

SILENE
S. caroliniana (wild pink); *S. quadrifida, also called S. alpestris* (alpine catchfly); *S. schafta* (Schafta campion)

Thriving in dry, sandy soils in open woodlands and alpine meadows, these three sprawling wildflowers provide dependable summer color on stone walls, rocky slopes or gravelly moraines. All three are perennials with soft, hairy, lance-shaped leaves and blunt-tipped petals like those of the garden pink. They spread slowly on deep fleshy roots.

The wild pink forms compact mounds 5 to 12 inches high. Its blue-green leaves are 3 to 5 inches long and its 1-inch white or pink flowers bloom in loose clusters at the ends of jointed stems in early summer. The alpine catchfly is creeping in habit and forms dense mats 6 to 12 inches high. It has slightly sticky leaves and stems and star-shaped white flowers, ¼ inch across, with notched tips. These bloom in loose clusters for about a month in summer. One variety, Florepleno, has double flowers. Schafta campion is also an alpine species. It grows in rosettes, forming dense 6-inch-high tufts of light-green leaves. The 1- to 2-inch flowers, in shades of rose and purple, appear singly or in pairs and bloom profusely from late summer into fall.

HOW TO GROW. Wild pink, alpine catchfly and Schafta campion are hardy in Zones 4-8 and grow in soil with a pH of 5.5 to 7.0. Wild pink grows in either sun or partial shade and does best in a sandy or rocky soil. Alpine catchfly grows best in sun and thrives in a deep, moist, well-drained soil. Schafta campion grows in either sun or partial shade and also does best in a deep, moist, well-drained soil. All three plants are easily grown from seed. Sow seeds in a cold frame in early spring, covering them with ⅛ inch of soil. Transplant seedlings when they are large enough to handle, spacing them 6 to 8 inches apart. Or divide plants in the spring. Wild pink may also be started from root cuttings, and Schafta campion from cuttings of young shoots, both taken in summer and rooted in a cold frame in sandy soil.

SILVER MOUND ARTEMISIA See *Artemisia*
SNAIL SAXIFRAGE See *Saxifraga*
SPIKE HEATH See *Bruckenthalia*
SPRING BEAUTY See *Claytonia*
SPRING HEATH See *Erica*
SPRUCE See *Picea*
SQUAWBERRY See *Mitchella*
SQUIRREL CORN See *Dicentra*
STEMLESS GENTIAN See *Gentiana*
STONECROP, SIEBOLD See *Sedum*
STRAWBERRY SAXIFRAGE See *Saxifraga*
SUENDERMANN DRYAD See *Dryas*
SWEET WOODRUFF See *Asperula*

T

THREE-TOOTHED CINQUEFOIL See *Potentilla*
THRIFT See *Armeria*

TRILLIUM

T. erectum (purple trillium); *T. grandiflorum* (great white trillium); *T. nivale* (dwarf white trillium)

Trilliums are spring-blooming wildflowers. Of more than 30 species, these three are recommended for rock gardens. All trilliums grow from thick rhizomes that spread laterally just below the soil level; some produce offsets to form clumps of plants. Leaves and flowers grow from a single stem and, as the name implies, there are three leaves per stem and each flower has three petals, three sepals and a three-celled berry.

The purple trillium grows about a foot high and bears reddish-brown flowers 1 to 3 inches across that look purple in some lighting but more often are closer in color to maroon. Great white trillium, the largest of the trilliums and the easiest to grow, has pure white flowers 3 inches across; they turn pale pink as they mature. It is somewhat taller than the purple trillium, growing 8 to 16 inches high, and a single rhizome may produce up to eight stems. Its leaves are a clear deep green; in some forms the flowers are double. Dwarf white trillium is a miniature version of the great white trillium; it grows only 4 to 5 inches high and its flowers are only 1 or 2 inches across.

HOW TO GROW. Trilliums are hardy in Zones 3-8 and thrive in a moist, well-drained, slightly acid soil, rich in humus. For the purple trillium, the acidity can range from pH 4.5 to 6.0; the great white and dwarf white trilliums do best in a range of pH 6.0 to 7.0. Plant them in the fall, setting the rhizomes 5 to 8 inches apart and 2 to 4 inches deep, with the buds of next year's growth facing upward. Propagate by dividing the rhizomes in the fall.

TROUT LILY See *Erythronium*

TSUGA

T. canadensis 'Cole'; *T. canadensis* 'Jervis'; *T. canadensis* 'Lewisii'; *T. canadensis* 'Minima' (all called dwarf Canadian hemlock)

The dwarf Canadian hemlocks include more than 75 cultivated varieties, among them some of the smallest conifers known. These shallow-rooted plants are often found growing in marshy bogs, and they are suitable for similarly cool, moist rock-garden situations. All of them have graceful, curving branches and flat, glossy, dark green needles, ⅜ inch long, with white bands on the underside.

Cole's hemlock is completely prostrate. When it is planted near rocks, the slender, limber stems drape over and around the rough terrain, forming a broad mat 2 to 6 inches tall and 2 to 3 feet wide. In a year, its branches will grow 4 to 8 inches and, with age, the main branches at the center will become bare. Lewisii is an upright dwarf, growing an inch a year to reach a height of 3 feet in 15 years. Its foliage is a deeper green than that of most Canadian hemlocks, and the needles are completely white on the underside.

Jervis is a compact shrub with gnarled, short branches and needles clustered densely and irregularly along the branches, giving the plant an asymmetrical silhouette. It grows less than an inch a year, reaching 12 to 15 inches. Minima is a low, spreading shrub with tiered branches that droop at the tips so the plant forms a softly rounded mound. It has the advantage of holding its needles for many years and thus its shape as it ages. With a maximum height of 3 feet and a spread to 10 feet, it is best suited to large rock gardens.

PURPLE TRILLIUM
Trillium erectum

DWARF CANADIAN HEMLOCK
Tsuga canadensis 'Cole'

For climate zones and frost dates, see maps, pages 150-151.

HOW TO GROW. Dwarf Canadian hemlocks are hardy in Zones 2-8. They grow best in sun but will tolerate partial shade, and they thrive in a cool, moist, well-drained acid soil with a pH of 5.5 to 6.5. They are susceptible to damage from polluted air, summer heat and drying winter winds. Water plants deeply during droughts. Plant hemlocks in either autumn or spring, preferably in a location where they will be given protection from winter winds.

TWINLEAF See *Jeffersonia*
TWO-ROW STONECROP See *Sedum*

V

VERNAL IRIS See *Iris*
VIRGINIA SPRING BEAUTY See *Claytonia*

W

WALL ROCK CRESS See *Arabis*
WANDFLOWER See *Galax*
WESTERN BLEEDING HEART See *Dicentra*
WHITE CINQUEFOIL See *Potentilla*
WILD GINGER, CANADA See *Asarum*
WILD PINK See *Silene*
WINE CUP See *Callirhoe*
WINELEAF CINQUEFOIL See *Potentilla*
WOOD ANEMONE, EUROPEAN See *Anemone*
WOODRUFF See *Asperula*
WOOLLY YARROW See *Achillea*

Y

YARROW, WOOLLY See *Achillea*
YELLOW ADDER'S-TONGUE See *Erythronium*
YELLOW CORYDALIS See *Corydalis*

CAPE PONDWEED
Aponogeton distachyus

Bog and water plants

A

ANDREWS GENTIAN See *Gentiana*

APONOGETON
A. distachyus (water hawthorn, Cape pondweed)

Water hawthorn is excellent for mild-climate ponds and pools with still or slowly moving water. Its bright green oblong leaves, 4 inches or more long, float on the surface, supported by a long underwater leaf stalk that rises from a fat, tuber-like rhizome; in bright sun the leaves sometimes have maroon or purple markings. In summer a profusion of waxy, sweet-scented flowers bursts into bloom on V-shaped flower spikes, each fork of which is 2 to 4 inches long. The flowers continue to appear well into fall and sometimes into the winter. They are normally white when they first open, gradually turning green as they age, although plants occasionally have pink or dark rose flowers, and in shallow water, 2 to 4 inches deep, white flowers become tinged with red. In very mild climates, the foliage stays green all year; the plant is a perennial, spreads moderately fast and may eventually cover an area 2 to 3 feet in diameter.

HOW TO GROW. Water hawthorn is hardy in Zones 9 and 10 and does well in full sun or open shade. It grows best in neutral or slightly acid soil with a pH of 7.0 to 8.0. Plant rhizomes in the spring, setting them directly in the bottom of a pond, 6 inches apart, or in containers; if the pond is small, containers are preferable, since they restrict growth. Ideally, rhizomes should be barely covered with water at the start but should eventually be 6 to 24 inches below the surface. To keep plants from seeding themselves, cut off faded flowers. Propagate by separating offsets from the rhizomes or by sowing seeds as soon as they are ripe. Scatter seeds on top of 2 to 3 inches of soil in a container that will hold water, then cover the soil with 4 to 6 inches of water. Keep at temperatures of 55° to 60° until seedlings sprout. When rhizomes are about pea-sized, plant them outdoors to get flowers the following year. Water hawthorn can also be started by dividing old rhizomes, but they grow very slowly.

ARROWHEAD See *Sagittaria*

B

BLIND GENTIAN See *Gentiana*
BULRUSH See *Cyperus*

C

CALLA
C. palustris (water arum, wild calla)

The water arum flourishes in bog gardens and shallow pools, and is a useful plant for hiding unsightly pool edges of concrete or mud. These aquatic perennials creep in and out of the water, their glossy heart-shaped leaves, up to 6 inches long, rising on 8- to 12-inch stems from long underwater rhizomes. Beginning in the second summer, many 2-inch-long flowers bloom just above the leaves; each looks like a miniature calla lily, with a white petal-like spathe surrounding a yellow knob-shaped spadix. The latter contains the true flowers. In fall, bright red berries cover the spadix. The water arum multiplies fairly rapidly and is often fertilized by snails that laboriously crawl up and down the stems of one flower after another, attracted by a rather unpleasant smell.

HOW TO GROW. Water arum is hardy in Zones 2-9. It does best in full sun in an acid muddy soil with a pH of 5.0 to 6.5. It needs still water; running water disturbs its roots. Set out plants in spring, placing them under 2 to 6 inches of water with the leaves above water level. In northern areas where the shallow roots may be killed by deep frost, water arum must be dug up in winter and stored indoors. Propagate by dividing the rhizomes after the flowers fade or by separating the seeds from the pulpy berries and planting them immediately in a moist mixture of sphagnum moss and topsoil.

CALTHA
C. palustris (marsh marigold, cowslip)

A good plant for stream banks and wet bog gardens, marsh marigold will thrive even in swiftly flowing water, held fast by deep, tangled roots. Its hollow stems, 8 to 24 inches tall, bear heart-shaped leaves, 2 to 7 inches wide. In spring, clusters of cup-shaped waxy yellow flowers, 1 to 2 inches wide, bloom on separate stalks along the stems. One variety, Alba, has white flowers, while another, *C. palustris monstrosa plena,* bears large double flowers. Marsh marigolds spread moderately fast and are perennials, but the entire plant dies to the ground by midsummer. Because they need wet soil only during active growth, they are excellent for gardens that are soggy in spring but dry in summer.

HOW TO GROW. Marsh marigold is hardy in Zones 3-8 and does best in full sun but will tolerate open shade. It thrives in a moist, humus-rich, acid soil with a pH of 5.0 to 7.0. Set out plants in spring, spacing them 9 to 12 inches apart and under 3 to 6 inches of water. During the spring growing season, keep the soil wet. Propagate by dividing root clumps either before flowers appear in early spring or when plants are

WATER ARUM
Calla palustris

Height 8 to 24 inches

MARSH MARIGOLD
Caltha palustris

For climate zones and frost dates, see maps, pages 150-151.

AQUATIC CANNA
Canna 'Erebus'

Height 6 to 10 feet

UMBRELLA PLANT
Cyperus alternifolius

dormant in summer. Except for double forms, which do not breed true, new plants can also be started from seeds sown in early summer, as soon as they are ripe. Seed-grown plants often do not bloom until the second year.

CANNA
C. glauca L. (aquatic canna); *C. glauca L.* hybrids

Like its land-based relative, the aquatic canna is a tall plant with thick stems, upright foliage and flower spikes that open gradually all summer long along the tops of the stems. In its species form, *C. glauca L.,* it grows 3 feet high, with relatively small, pale yellow flowers, 1½ to 2 inches across, and narrow lance-shaped leaves. When crossed with terrestrial cannas, however, the leaves are broader, 5 to 6 inches wide; the flowers are larger, 4 inches across, and they bloom more profusely, in more vivid colors.

The hybrids range from 5 to 6 feet tall and have flowers 4 inches wide. Their foliage varies in length from 1½ to 2 feet and is 5 to 6 inches wide. Endeavor has bright red flowers and foliage edged with a narrow purple margin. Erebus has salmon pink flowers and leaves with translucent white margins. Ra bears bright yellow flowers and has white-bordered leaves, while Taney, also with white-bordered leaves, has burnt orange flowers. All of them grow from rhizomes.

HOW TO GROW. Aquatic cannas are hardy in Zones 9 and 10. They need full sun, water temperatures between 65° and 75° and soil enriched with 8 ounces of 10-10-10 aquatic fertilizer per bushel. Plant them in containers, covering both rhizomes and soil with a 1-inch layer of sand. Lower the containers into the water so the rhizomes are between 4 and 6 inches beneath the surface. In fall, remove plants from the outdoor pool for the winter. Keep them in tubs of water in a warm greenhouse, or lift the roots and store them in moist peat moss in a cool, well-ventilated place. Fertilize aquatic cannas annually before returning them to the outdoor pool by planting them in rich soil. Propagate by dividing rhizomes in the fall, as they are lifted from the pool.

CAPE PONDWEED See *Aponogeton*
CARDINAL FLOWER See *Lobelia*
CATTAIL See *Typha*
CLOSED GENTIAN See *Gentiana*
COWSLIP See *Caltha*

CYPERUS
C. alternifolius (umbrella plant); *C. papyrus* (papyrus, bulrush, paper plant)

The umbrella plant and papyrus are semiaquatic plants, growing either in water or at the water's edge. Both species are extremely tall, papyrus sometimes rising to a height of 10 feet, but both are also available in dwarf varieties, labeled Nanus, which are likely to be more appropriate for a garden pool. Both plants are sedges, relatives of grasses, with essentially leafless stems—the leaves are there but they sheathe the stems and are scarcely visible. At the tops of the stems, the plants bear wide-spreading clusters of leaflike sepals and inconspicuous spikelets of flowers that change from yellow or green to light brown. The umbrella plant is 2 to 4 feet tall and has dark green leaf-sheathed stems; the narrow sepals that crown its top are 4 to 12 inches long. In addition to the Nanus dwarf varieties, there is also an umbrella plant with white-bordered leaves, Variegatus. Papyrus grows 6 to 10 feet tall, with leaflike sepals up to 12 inches long. Its flower spikelets end in drooping threadlike extensions, called rays, 12 to 18 inches long. Like grasses, these sedges rise in clumps from masses of roots.

HOW TO GROW. Umbrella plant and papyrus are hardy only in Zones 9 and 10, but grow either in sun or partial shade. They need water temperatures of 64° to 70° and a water depth of 6 inches. Plant them in heavy topsoil, setting them 18 to 24 inches apart; if planted in containers, choose pots or tubs of similar widths and depths of 8 to 12 inches. Propagate by dividing roots in spring.

D

DEW THREAD See *Drosera*

DROSERA

D. filiformis (threadleaf sundew, dew thread); *D. intermedia,* also called *D. longifolia; D. rotundifolia* (roundleaf sundew)

For variety's sake, no bog garden is complete without at least one insectivorous plant such as sundew. The leaves of these tiny perennials form a rosette and are covered with sticky hairs that trap insects. Once their prey is ensnarled, the leaves curl up and secrete an acid to digest their victims, then unfold again. When wet, the foliage sparkles in the sun as though dotted with dew. In summer, short flower stems slowly uncurl from the center of the rosette, each stem being capped by small, five-petaled flowers ¼ to 1 inch long. Threadleaf sundew forms tufts of grasslike leaves, 4 to 10 inches long, with purple hairs; its purple flowers cap 3- to 9-inch-tall stems. The variety Tracyi has green hairs. *D. intermedia* has wedge-shaped leaves, up to 1½ inches long, with red hairs; they form a clump about 6 inches high. Its flower stems, 1 to 10 inches tall, bear very tiny white flowers. Roundleaf sundew foliage becomes only ¾ to 2 inches tall; it has round leaves with red hairs and produces flower stems 2 to 12 inches tall, which carry small pink or white flowers. Sundews spread rapidly to make thick carpets.

HOW TO GROW. *D. intermedia* and roundleaf sundew are hardy in Zones 3-9; threadleaf sundew is hardy in Zones 5-7 but the variety Tracyi will grow as far south as Zone 9. All thrive in full sun and very wet or muddy acid soil, pH 4.0 to 5.0, which is rich in peat moss or sphagnum moss. Set out plants in spring, spacing them 4 to 5 inches apart. Place the rhizomes in shallow depressions and barely cover them with soil. Keep constantly moist. Sundews seed themselves readily and may be propagated from seed or by dividing rhizomes. Sow seeds in a pot and keep the soil constantly moist by standing the pot in a dish filled with water.

E

EICHHORNIA

E. crassipes (water hyacinth)

Decorative, ornamental floaters, water hyacinths grow in dense mats. In several Southern states, they became such a menace to navigation that Congress prohibited the sale or transportation of these plants across state lines. However, when grown in a warm-water pool or tub where they can be controlled, these attractive aquatic plants offer an intriguing display of lovely flowers and strange foliage. The water hyacinth grows 6 to 9 inches tall and ranges from 6 to 12 inches in diameter. The shiny light-green oval leaves, 2 to 5 inches wide, have curiously swollen, spongy bases filled with air pockets that give the plants buoyancy; the leaves rise from a common source, in rosette formation. Delicate clusters of pale lavender flowers, 3 to 4 inches long, bloom at the end of 6-inch stalks that grow from the center of each rosette. The uppermost petal of each flower bears a distinctive, tear-shaped yellow patch. The water hyacinth's feathery, purple-white roots, usually 12 to 18 inches long, trail in the water and provide spawning grounds for fish.

For climate zones and frost dates, see maps, pages 150-151.

ROUNDLEAF SUNDEW
Drosera rotundifolia

WATER HYACINTH
Eichhornia crassipes

HOW TO GROW. Water hyacinths will die if exposed to only a few degrees of frost, so they are suitable for permanent planting outdoors only in Zones 9 and 10. The plants require full sun and plenty of space. Two inches of rich bottom soil and a water depth of 6 to 18 inches is ideal. No planting is necessary; simply float water hyacinths on the water after frost danger has passed. Most gardeners purchase new plants each spring. Propagate by root division or by separating runners from the parent plant, but this is rarely necessary. Indeed, thinning out excess plants will be the prime concern.

G

GENTIAN See *Gentiana*

GENTIANA
G. andrewsii (Andrews gentian, closed gentian, blind gentian)

Andrews gentian is a bog plant that thrives in moist woodland gardens. It grows 1 to 2 feet tall, has lance-shaped leaves 2 to 3½ inches long, and in late summer and early fall bears candelabra-like clusters of upright flowers cradled by circles of leaves. The bottle-shaped flowers, up to 1½ inches long, never open; they are usually purplish-blue with white tips but in rare instances may be all white. These perennials have deep, gnarled taproots and spread moderately fast.

HOW TO GROW. The Andrews gentian is hardy in Zones 3-8 and does well in partial shade or full sun. It grows best in well-drained, moist, slightly acid soil, pH 5.5 to 6.5, enriched with leaf mold or peat moss, but it will also tolerate more neutral soil. Set out plants in the fall, spacing them 8 to 12 inches apart. Place the roots about 1 inch below the soil surface. Keep the soil moist at all times. Propagate by removing offsets from the roots of established plants in the spring, or by sowing seeds in the fall as soon as they are ripe. Sow seeds in flats and sprinkle finely chopped sphagnum moss over them. Transplant seedlings to the garden the following spring for flowers in three years.

GLOBEFLOWER See *Trollius*

H

HAWTHORN, WATER See *Aponogeton*

HYDROCLEYS
H. nymphoides (water poppy)

Water poppies are flowering shallow-water plants; their three-petaled blooms resemble those of the unrelated California poppy. Small tender perennials, they thrive in warm-weather pools and indoor/outdoor tubs. Their shiny green oval leaves, each 1 to 3 inches in diameter, resemble the foliage of miniature waterlilies. Deep yellow flowers 2 to 3 inches wide bloom profusely throughout the summer; each flower, however, lasts only for a day. Water poppies grow from rhizomes and are rapid spreaders with creeping stems that root at their nodes.

HOW TO GROW. Water poppies can be grown permanently outdoors only in frost-free areas of Zones 9 and 10. Elsewhere, restrict them to summer pools or to aboveground containers that can be moved indoors. The plants require full sun. Rooted stems or rhizomes must not be set out until all danger of frost is past. In warm-water natural ponds, plant them directly into the mud at the margin, with no more than 1½ feet of water covering them. In man-made pools, use containers filled with several inches of garden soil topped by an inch of sand. Submerge the containers in 6 to 9 inches of water. For freestanding tubs, fill them three quarters full of garden soil, again adding an inch of sand, then warm water to the brim; insert rhizomes as for natural ponds. As cold weather approaches, move the tubs indoors to a sunny spot. Also bring container-grown plants indoors, setting them under water. Propagate by rhizome division in spring.

I

INDIAN PINK See *Lobelia*

IRIS

I. kaempferi (Japanese iris); *I. laevigata* (rabbit-ear iris)

These irises, similar in appearance, are suited to slightly different areas of the water garden. The Japanese iris thrives in bogs and does well in locations that are wet in spring and summer but dry in winter. Rabbit-ear iris flourishes in shallow water and is a useful plant for the edges of pools and ponds. Both of these hardy perennials bloom in summer and grow up to 2 feet tall, with swordlike leaves that are almost identical except for the conspicuous center rib of the Japanese iris leaf. Branching sprays of two or three large flowers dance above the foliage in summer and sometimes again in fall. These distinctive flowers have three erect petals called standards and three large outer petal-like sepals called falls. Neither species is bearded.

Japanese iris has large flowers, 4 to 10 inches wide, with short standards and broad falls that resemble butterfly wings. The species has reddish-purple flowers with yellow blotches but other varieties come with single and double flowers in blue, purple, pink and white, veined in contrasting colors. One such is the rose-pink Kagari Bi, with veins of a deeper hue. Higo is an excellent strain with 8- to 10-inch-wide blooms whose petals are remarkably resistant to high wind. Rabbit-ear iris has 4- to 6-inch-wide flowers with standards and falls of equal size. While the species has deep blue flowers with white or yellow blotches, varieties may have all-white, rose or purple flowers, and one variegated form, Colchesterensis, bears white-edged blue flowers. Both Japanese and rabbit-ear irises form clumps with fibrous roots.

HOW TO GROW. Japanese and rabbit-ear iris are hardy in Zones 4-9. They grow best in full sun and a moist or wet acid soil with a pH of 5.5 to 6.5; however, the roots of Japanese iris must be dry in winter. Set out plants in spring, spacing them 1 to 1½ feet apart. Japanese iris roots should be set so that their tops are 2 to 3 inches below the soil level, rabbit-ear iris roots so that their tops are 2 to 3 inches below water level. Sprinkle peat moss or compost around the base of Japanese iris and fertilize it once a year in early spring with liquid manure. Do not fertilize rabbit-ear iris. Divide plants every three or four years to prevent crowding. Propagate by dividing established plants in spring.

L

LOBELIA

L. cardinalis (cardinal flowers, Indian pink); *L. siphilitica* (great blue lobelia)

Both cardinal flower and great blue lobelia grow naturally in marshy ground and are especially useful for banks of brooks and streams; cardinal flower will even hold fast in running water. These perennials are usually 1 to 3 feet tall, with stiff stems and thin, serrated leaves 2 to 4 inches long. Their flower spikes carry tiny tubular flowers with five lobes each: the two top lobes flare outward like rabbit ears, while the bottom three lobes resemble a hanging lip. Cardinal flower produces 2-inch-long red blooms from midsummer to fall; great blue lobelia bears 1-inch-long white-tipped blue-violet flowers in midsummer. Occasionally both species produce white-flowered varieties, and one variety of great blue

Height up to 2 feet

JAPANESE IRIS
Iris kaempferi 'Kagari Bi'

Height 1 to 3 feet

CARDINAL FLOWER
Lobelia cardinalis

For climate zones and frost dates, see maps, pages 150-151.

lobelia has burgundy flowers. Lobelias spread very rapidly from shallow, fibrous roots and usually seed themselves.

HOW TO GROW. Lobelias grow in Zones 3-9 in full sun or open shade. They do best in a wet, humus-rich soil with a pH of 5.5 to 7.0. Set out plants in late spring, spacing them 8 to 12 inches apart. During dry periods, mulch plants to keep them moist; in northern zones where the ground freezes, mulch in winter with a covering of leaves. Propagate by dividing roots in spring or fall or from stem cuttings taken in spring or early summer before flowering. Both species can be started from seeds sown in flats in spring or fall and moved as seedlings to the garden the following spring.

LOTUS See *Nelumbo*

M

MARSH MARIGOLD See *Caltha*

N

NELUMBO

N. nucifera (lotus, sacred lotus, Hindu lotus, East Indian lotus, sacred bean)

The stately lotus is the most exotic of all water-garden plants. It produces huge, hauntingly aromatic 12-inch-wide pink, rose, yellow or white flowers that open from elegantly pointed buds in mid- to late summer atop 3- to 8-foot stems. Each flower takes three days to open fully, opening each morning and closing each afternoon. When its petals fall an unusual brown bowl-shaped seed pod is revealed, flat-topped and pierced with holes, like the nozzle of a watering can. Silvery blue-green parasol-shaped leaves, 1 to 3 feet in diameter, float on the water or flare out 3 to 6 feet above the surface. Their waxy coating causes raindrops to slide off like quicksilver. Lotuses grow from brittle banana-shaped tubers that send out prolific lateral runners that may become 20 to 30 feet long in one season. Unless planted in large ponds, lotuses should be confined to containers.

HOW TO GROW. Lotuses are hardy in Zones 4-10 but will only survive the winter outdoors if their roots do not freeze. The plants do best in full sun and for good bloom require water temperatures of 60° to 70°. In large ponds, plant lotus tubers directly in the bottom soil, under 1 to 2 feet of water. Alternatively, roll the seeds in clay and drop them into the water. For container-grown plants use bushel-sized tubs, filled with heavy garden soil, preferably mixed with ¼ part clay; for each bushel add ½ to 1 pound of commercial fertilizer recommended for aquatic plants. Moisten the soil thoroughly, make a shallow depression, and place the tuber in it, taking care not to touch the growing tip. Cover it with about 1 inch of soil, leaving about ½ inch of the growing tip exposed. Top with an inch of sand, leaving the growing tip exposed. Submerge containers in 2 inches of water; as the plant grows, gradually lower it to a depth of 6 to 12 inches.

Feed lotuses with two tablets of aquatic fertilizer every month during the growing season. During the winter, protect lotuses in shallow pools or severe-weather areas by covering the pool with wood or canvas, topped by a 3-inch layer of straw, leaves or salt hay. Or move the containers to a well-ventilated spot where the temperatures remain between 35° and 45°, keeping the soil thoroughly moist. Some gardeners prefer to cut off the foliage and store the tubers in damp, clean sand. Every two years, dig up container-grown plants in spring; cut away old sections and replant healthy portions with several growing tips attached. Propagate lotuses by dividing tubers in spring, or plant seeds in pans of sandy soil submerged in water heated to 60°.

SACRED LOTUS
Nelumbo nucifera

NYMPHAEA

N. colorata, also called *N. polychroma; N.* hardy hybrids; *N.* tropical hybrids (all called waterlilies)

Waterlilies have been hybridized into so many forms that there is a waterlily for any garden pool, no matter what its size or the color preferences of its owner. There are pygmy waterlilies, scarcely 2 inches across, and giant varieties with 14-inch flowers. The blooms, which are cup shaped or star shaped, usually last three or four days and come in shades and combinations of pink, yellow, apricot, red, lavender, purple, blue and white. The leaves, called lily pads, range in width from 2 to 18 inches and may be round, indented or heart shaped. Though normally green, they may in some varieties be reddish-brown or purple, and they are often streaked or speckled with contrasting colors.

For practical and decorative purposes, waterlilies are commonly divided into two main classes, hardy and tropical, and tropical lilies are further subdivided into night-blooming and day-blooming varieties. Hardy lilies bloom only in the daytime. Both are perennials, but in northern gardens hardy waterlilies can remain outdoors all winter if ice does not form around roots, while tropical lilies generally are grown as annuals and replaced each year. In most areas, hardy lilies bloom throughout the summer, bearing the flowers at water level on short stalks. Tropical lilies bloom from summer well into the autumn, bearing their flowers on stalks that rise 6 to 18 inches above the surface of the water. Their flowers tend to be more waxy than those of hardy lilies, and their leaves are more prominently marked. Even when they are grown in containers, they spread rapidly to cover wider areas than the hardy lilies.

Among the best of the hardy lilies are Attraction, the largest of all red waterlilies, with flowers up to 10 inches across; and Comanche, the largest of what are often called the changeables; i.e., its 5-inch blooms open as apricot-rose and gradually darken to a deep coppery bronze. Other recommended hardy lilies are Helvola, a miniature lily with cream-colored 2- to 2½-inch flowers and olive-green leaves speckled with red; Chromatella, with 4- to 5-inch chrome yellow flowers; Paul Hariot, another changeable whose 4-inch blooms open as light-yellow with pink overtones and darken to reddish-orange; Pink Sensation, with 6-inch pale pink flowers; Sunrise, with 8- to 9-inch sulfur-yellow flowers and olive-green leaves marked for two days with maroon; and Virginalis, an 8- to 9-inch white waterlily with an exceptionally long blooming season, up to nine months.

In the category of tropical day-blooming lilies the most popular varieties include Director George T. Moore, whose deep blue-purple flowers, 8 to 10 inches across, are remarkable for the rarity of their color; and General Pershing, a very fragrant lily with 8- to 10-inch pale pink flowers. Other day-blooming tropicals with large blooms are Isabelle Pring, pure white; Pink Platter, lilac; and Yellow Dazzler, chrome yellow. Among smaller versions of the day-blooming tropicals two recommended plants are St. Louis Gold, a yellow lily 4 to 5 inches across, and the species waterlily *N. colorata,* whose 4-inch flowers are bright blue tinged with mauve.

Night-blooming tropical waterlilies, which open at dusk and tend to remain open until the following noon, are as a group larger than their day-blooming relatives. Among recommended varieties, all with 9- to 12-inch flowers, are Emily Grant Hutchings, a pink lily; H. C. Haarstick, vivid red shading to pink with bronze-red leaves; and the fragrant Red Flare, fire-engine red with mahogany-colored leaves.

HOW TO GROW. Hardy and tropical waterlilies are grown together in the same pool in Zones 4-10, but hardy lilies

ATTRACTION WATERLILY
Nymphaea 'Attraction'

GEORGE T. MOORE WATERLILY
Nymphaea colorata 'Director George T. Moore'

For climate zones and frost dates, see maps, pages 150-151.

COMANCHE WATERLILY
Nymphaea 'Comanche'

EMILY GRANT HUTCHINGS WATERLILY
Nymphaea 'Emily Grant Hutchings'

survive the winter in these zones, while tropical lilies are considered annuals above Zone 8; both kinds bloom year round in Zones 9 and 10, though tropicals need a two- to three-week rest period. They all need five to eight hours of sun a day and grow best with a southern exposure. Still water is essential and, for tropical waterlilies, water temperatures should not drop below 70°; hardy lilies will flower at temperatures somewhat lower, 65°. The best planting medium is a heavy topsoil enriched with ½ pound of aquatic fertilizer per 12-quart container.

Set out hardy lilies in early spring, when water temperatures are between 50° and 55°; for tropical lilies wait until water temperatures have risen to 70°. Plant them directly in the bottom of the pool, setting the rhizomes or rootstocks just beneath the surface of the soil, with their bud tips exposed. Or plant them in containers suitable to the size of the lily—6 inches wide for the miniature varieties, 10 inches wide for medium-sized plants, 20 inches wide for the largest tropical lilies. Allow enough space between plants to accommodate their eventual sizes. A medium-sized waterlily plant is about 3 feet in diameter; giant waterlilies spread to fill an area 6 to 9 feet across. Cover the newly planted stock with water appropriate to its stage of growth. If growth has barely begun, the plants should be covered with only a few inches of water, so sunlight can reach the young buds. Once growth is established, lower the plant to its normal growing depth. Some varieties of waterlilies do well in very shallow or very deep water, but hardy lilies in general need 8 to 12 inches of water above them, tropical lilies 6 to 12 inches.

Waterlilies should be fed every two or three weeks during their period of bloom with a 4-8-5 or 5-10-5 aquatic plant fertilizer, usually applied, for convenience' sake, in the form of slow-release tablets. In general, tropical varieties need to be fed more often than hardy varieties. Remove decaying foliage regularly, and trim off faded flowers. In areas where winters are severe, cover the pool with boards and a layer of burlap, leaving an air space on the south edge if there are fish in the pool. Or move plants and their containers indoors, wrapping the containers in moist burlap and then plastic film to retain moisture. Store in a cool basement.

To propagate hardy lilies, wash soil off roots to locate growing tips; cut roots into 6- to 8-inch sections and replant. Most gardeners divide roots in spring or late summer. Propagating tropical lilies generally requires a greenhouse, and plants are usually purchased new each season.

P

PAPER PLANT See *Cyperus*
PAPYRUS See *Cyperus*
PICKEREL WEED See *Pontederia*

PISTIA
P. stratiotes (water lettuce, shellflower)

Water lettuce is a tender free-floating aquatic perennial. In the wild, these heat-loving plants are found in quiet ponds and streams, but they will flourish in warm-water outdoor pools. Water lettuce is grown for its iridescent blue-green foliage rather than for its inconspicuous green flowers. The velvety, heavily veined leaves form rosettes 6 inches wide, from which long, slender hairlike roots dangle in the water. When restricted, the plants will take root in soil, but as a rule they spin over the surface of the water in the slightest breeze. Water lettuce spreads on lateral runners.

HOW TO GROW. Water lettuce requires water temperatures of 70° to 80° and thus grows permanently in outdoor pools only in frost-free areas of Zones 9 and 10. Elsewhere, they must be treated as annuals and be replanted each year or moved to indoor pools where the necessary water temperature can be maintained. The plants grow best when they are shaded from direct sun at midday. To plant, simply float water lettuce on the surface of the water after the temperature has risen to 70°. The plants require no further attention other than an occasional thinning. If you move them indoors over the winter, plant them in 18- to 24-inch-wide containers with 6 inches of garden soil at the bottom, then fill to the brim with water; add more water as it evaporates and provide high humidity. To propagate, detach the small plants that form on the lateral runners, and float them in separate containers or on the water surface.

PONTEDERIA
P. cordata (pickerel weed)

In shallow streams throughout the eastern half of the United States, pickerel weed grows wild, its forest of sturdy stems providing a hiding place for the fish that gave it its common name. In the garden, pickerel weed is suitable for similar situations but it will also grow in boggy soil at the water's edge. One of the handsomest of aquatic plants, its dark green heart-shaped leaves, 10 inches long and 6 inches wide, sheathe stems that rise 1 to 4 feet tall. In summer and fall it bears dense 3- to 4-inch spikes of orchid-like blue-violet flowers. The plant spreads rapidly on creeping rhizomes, and if not confined in a container, may become an annoyance.

HOW TO GROW. Pickerel weed is hardy in Zones 3-9 and grows best in water temperatures between 60° and 70°. It needs slow-moving or still shallow water 6 to 12 inches deep. In spring, plant rhizomes on the surface of the soil; cover them with a stone until they are rooted. To propagate, divide rhizomes at any time during the growing season.

PRIMROSE See *Primula*

PRIMULA
P. beesiana (Bee's primrose); *P. bullesiana* (Bulle's primrose); *P. frondosa* (Balkan primrose); *P. japonica* (Japanese primrose)

All primroses need moisture to some degree but these four species have a special affinity for it and are widely used along the waterside. Balkan primrose, an alpine plant, is also suitable for scree gardens. The four are alike in being perennials, with oval, coarse-textured leaves and flowers that bloom in clusters 2 to 6 inches wide. But Bee's, Bulle's and the Japanese primrose have light-green leaves and produce their flower clusters in candelabra-like tiers along tall stems, while the low-growing Balkan primrose's blooms rest against its rosette of ground-hugging gray-green foliage. Bee's primrose grows 1½ to 2 feet tall, with 8-inch-long leaves; its ¾-inch flowers are rose-lilac with yellow centers and bloom in early summer. Bulle's primrose also flowers in early summer and is 1½ to 2 feet tall; its leaves are up to 12 inches long, and its ¾-inch flowers come in hues of pink, white, purple, orange and red. Balkan primrose grows only 2 to 5 inches tall, with 4-inch leaves and ½-inch rose-purple flowers with yellow centers. It blooms in the spring. Japanese primrose reaches a height of 2½ feet and bears several whorls of 1-inch white, pink, red or blue flowers from late spring until early summer. Primroses have deep taproots, spread rapidly and often seed themselves.

HOW TO GROW. Bee's, Bulle's and Balkan primroses are hardy in Zones 6-8; Japanese primrose is hardy in Zones 5-8. All do best in areas with cool, moist summers and prefer partial shade, but Japanese primrose can also tolerate some

WATER LETTUCE
Pistia stratiotes

Height 1 to 4 feet

PICKEREL WEED
Pontederia cordata

For climate zones and frost dates, see maps, pages 150-151.

Height up to 2½ feet

JAPANESE PRIMROSE
Primula japonica

Height up to 4 feet

OLD WORLD ARROWHEAD
Sagittaria sagittifolia

sun. They need a wet, well-drained, gritty acid soil, with a pH of 5.0 to 6.0, supplemented with peat moss or leaf mold. Set out plants in early summer, spacing them 6 to 12 inches apart. Keep moist at all times. In late fall, cover plants with a light mulch of hay or straw. Fertilize with dry manure, bone meal or a balanced fertilizer such as 10-10-10 in spring or fall. Propagate by dividing plant clumps after flowering or by moving offshoots. New plants are also easily started from seeds sown in the fall as soon as they are ripe and kept over the winter in a cold frame. Transplant to the garden the following spring. In mild climates Japanese primrose may act as a biennial, dying after two years; for a constant supply of flowers, sow seeds every year. All primroses need to be divided every two to three years to prevent overcrowding.

S

SACRED BEAN See *Nelumbo*

SAGITTARIA

S. montevidensis (giant arrowhead); *S. sagittifolia* (Old World arrowhead)

These tall aquatic perennials derive their name from the distinctive shape of the above-water leaves. (At water level the leaves are oval, and foliage growing underwater is slender and ribbon-like.) The giant and Old World arrowheads grow in boggy places in warm areas of Florida and California, at the edges of ponds, quiet streams or marshes. In colder regions, the giant arrowhead is grown as an annual in an outdoor pool or is wintered over in an indoor pool or tub. The Old World arrowhead, however, often will survive northern winters outdoors. Giant arrowheads may become 3 feet tall. Their aerial leaves are 1 to 3 feet in length with a pair of basal lobes nearly as long as the rest of the pointed blade. In late summer, whorls of 1- to 2-inch-wide white flowers with brownish-purple centers bloom in spikes on thick upright stalks. The less imposing Old World arrowhead grows only 2 feet tall with 2- to 8-inch aerial leaves. Its whorls of 1-inch-wide white flowers with speckled purple centers also bloom in late summer. Both plants grow in wet soil from fleshy, tuberous rootstocks; they multiply rapidly by means of underground runners and can become invasive.

HOW TO GROW. Old World arrowheads are hardy in Zones 5-10, but giant arrowheads grow permanently outdoors only in those areas of Zones 9 and 10 where temperatures do not fall below freezing or where their roots are planted below the frost line. Elsewhere, restrict their culture outdoors to summer pools or to indoor tubs and pools where the minimum winter temperature does not fall below 50°. Both species require full sun. Plant arrowheads in early spring, taking care not to damage their growing shoots. In permanent outdoor settings, push the tuberous roots 2 to 3 inches deep into the mud at the edge of the pond or into the bottom soil of the pool, spacing them 12 to 15 inches apart. In pool-grown containers, plant them 2 to 3 inches deep in 6 to 8 inches of garden loam fertilized with 4-8-5 or 5-10-5 aquatic fertilizer and topped with an inch of sand; then submerge them in 2 to 6 inches of water. In cold climate zones, bring outdoor giant arrowheads indoors before the first frost and store the tubers in moist sand until the following spring.

If arrowheads become invasive or become crowded, lift tubers and trim them to check growth. Propagate by tuber division in early spring, or sow seeds ¼ inch deep in soil-filled boxes placed in shallow water at 60° to 65°.

SHELLFLOWER See *Pistia*
SUNDEW See *Drosera*

T

TROLLIUS

T. laxus (spreading globeflower, American globeflower)

The spreading globeflower is a somewhat sprawling plant with weak, many-branched stems. It grows in swamps and bogs and is excellent for softening the edges of pools and streams. Its flower resembles that of the buttercup, but is much larger, 1 to 1½ inches across. It is composed of five or six spreading yellow or yellow-green sepals, surrounding a cluster of much more numerous petals that form a globe-shaped center. Spreading globeflower grows up to 2 feet high from a thick, fibrous root and has deeply cut leaves, 3 to 5 inches wide, with serrated edges. It blooms in spring and, after it has flowered, its leaves increase greatly in size.

HOW TO GROW. Spreading globeflower is hardy in Zones 3-9 and grows best in open shade. It needs a constantly moist, humus-enriched soil with a pH of 6.0 to 7.0. Plant sections of root 12 inches apart in spring or fall. Propagate in spring or fall by dividing roots of established plants, or start new plants from seed in a shady seedbed, transplanting them into the garden when they are large enough to handle.

TYPHA

T. angustifolia (narrow-leaved cattail, graceful cattail)

Stately, reedlike cattails, with the familiar, rigid, poker-shaped heads much used in dried arrangements, grow freely in swamps, marshes and bogs. In water gardening, these tall, erect perennials are handsome additions to large pools and ponds as accent or background specimens. Because of their size and the fact that they are most effective when grown in masses, the plants are not suitable for tub culture or small pools. The narrow-leaved cattail usually becomes 2 to 5 feet tall. It develops stiff green straplike leaves 18 to 24 inches in length and about ½ inch in width. They are frequently used in chair caning and basket weaving. The cylindrical brown flower heads, borne in summer at the ends of swordlike stalks, measure from ⅝ inch to 1¼ inches in diameter and 6 to 8 inches in length. Cattails grow from thick underground rhizomes and are vigorous spreaders that can become weedy.

HOW TO GROW. Narrow-leaved cattails are hardy in wetland areas of Zones 2-10, particularly in the eastern and central states. Plant short pieces of the rhizome with young shoots attached in early spring. In naturalized ponds, set the rhizome divisions 1 to 3 feet apart, 1 inch below soil level and covered with no more than 12 inches of water. In formal pools, plant rhizomes in tubs or, alternatively, portion off a section of the pool with a retainer to keep cattails within bounds. Plant the cattails just below the soil's surface in soil 6 to 12 inches deep and cover with an inch of sand. Cattails in pools grow best submerged in 2 to 5 inches of water. They require no further care except to trim the rhizomes back if the cattails grow beyond their allotted space. You may propagate additional plants by rhizome division in fall or spring, or you may collect and plant seeds in the autumn in pots of rich soil set in a few inches of warm water.

U

UMBRELLA PLANT See *Cyperus*

W

WATER ARUM See *Calla*
WATER HAWTHORN See *Aponogeton*
WATER HYACINTH See *Eichhornia*
WATER LETTUCE See *Pistia*
WATERLILY See *Nymphaea*
WATER POPPY See *Hydrocleys*

For climate zones and frost dates, see maps, pages 150-151.

Height up to 2 feet

SPREADING GLOBEFLOWER
Trollius laxus

Height 4 to 6 feet

NARROW-LEAVED CATTAIL
Typha angustifolia

Climate notes for rock and water gardeners

Since rock and water gardens can be created from such a wide array of plants—including alpines, shrubs, bulbs, herbs, ferns, rushes and waterlilies—you should have little difficulty in selecting a combination that will thrive wherever you live. To help you identify plants suited to your area, the preceding encyclopedia gives the climate zones where each will grow. The map below shows the location of each of the 10 zones, determined according to the minimum winter temperature in different parts of the United States and Canada.

Of course, choosing plants is only one phase of rock and water gardening. To schedule other tasks, consult the maps on the opposite page for average dates of the frosts in your area.

Since rock and water gardens require much preparation before plants can be installed, plan to have a pool cleaned or a rock-garden construction project completed by the time of the last frost. Then, in early spring, you can devote undivided attention to planting the rock garden, perhaps adding alpines, conifers or ferns. As the sun gradually warms the pool, add aquatic planting to your gardening calendar, starting with marginals and hardy waterlilies, and then adding tender tropicals when the water reaches 70°. Finish late-fall pruning of rock plants and marginals before a killing frost collapses their foliage. And before the pool is crusted with ice, move container-planted lilies to protect the rhizomes from freezing.

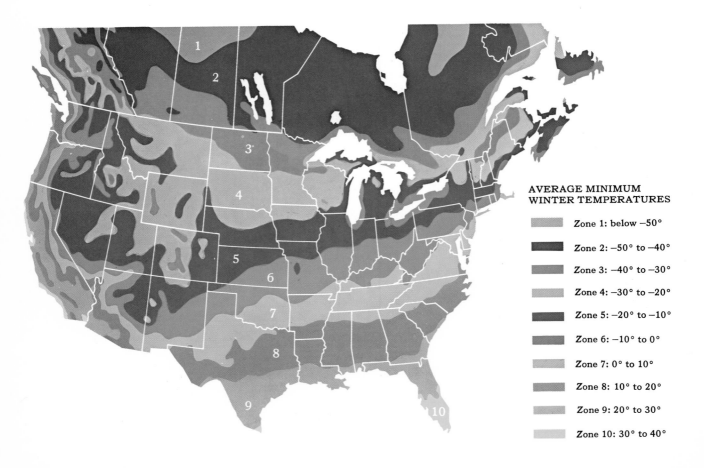

AVERAGE MINIMUM WINTER TEMPERATURES

Zone 1: below −50°

Zone 2: −50° to −40°

Zone 3: −40° to −30°

Zone 4: −30° to −20°

Zone 5: −20° to −10°

Zone 6: −10° to 0°

Zone 7: 0° to 10°

Zone 8: 10° to 20°

Zone 9: 20° to 30°

Zone 10: 30° to 40°

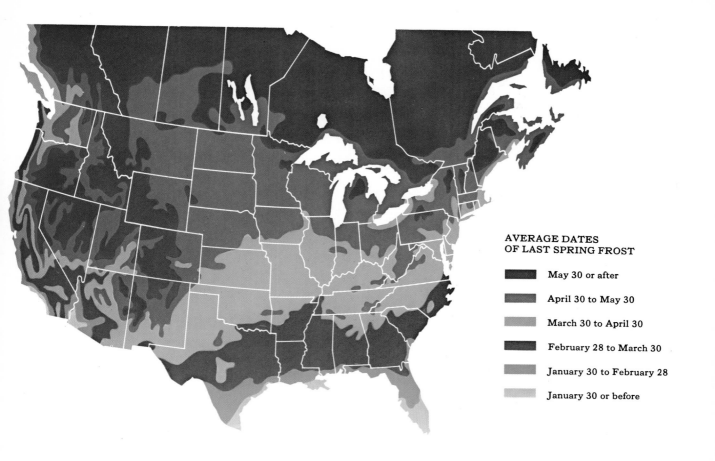

AVERAGE DATES
OF LAST SPRING FROST

May 30 or after

April 30 to May 30

March 30 to April 30

February 28 to March 30

January 30 to February 28

January 30 or before

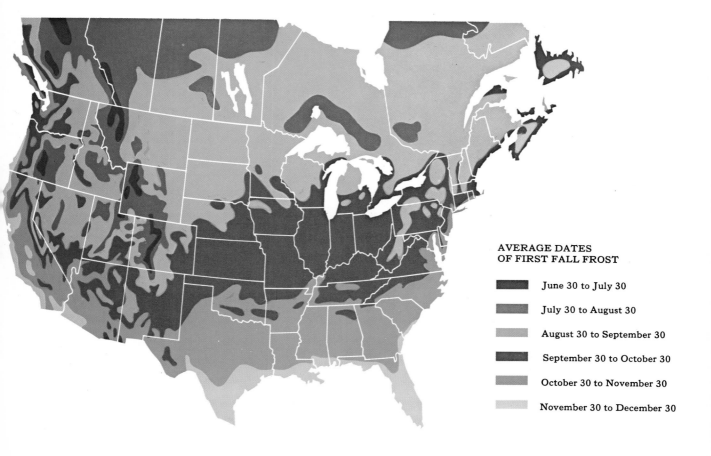

AVERAGE DATES
OF FIRST FALL FROST

June 30 to July 30

July 30 to August 30

August 30 to September 30

September 30 to October 30

October 30 to November 30

November 30 to December 30

Characteristics of 82 rock-garden plants

Listed below for quick reference are the species illustrated in Chapter 5.

Species	PLANT HEIGHT				LIGHT NEEDS			GROWTH HABIT			SPECIAL TRAITS				FLOWER COLOR				FLOWER SEASON					
	Under 6 inches	6 to 12 inches	1 to 3 feet	Over 3 feet	Shade	Partial shade	Full sun	Upright	Spreading	Trailing	Flowers	Distinctive foliage	Evergreen	Decorative fruit	White to green	Yellow to orange	Pink to red	Blue to purple	Spring	Summer	Fall	Acid	Neutral	Alkaline
ACHILLEA TOMENTOSA (woolly yarrow)	•	•				•	•				•	•				•				•		•		
AJUGA REPTANS (bugleweed)	•	•			•	•	•	•			•	•					•	•	•			•		
ALLIUM MOLY (golden garlic)		•				•	•	•			•					•				•		•		
ALYSSUM SAXATILE (basket-of-gold)		•					•				•					•		•				•	•	
ANACYCLUS DEPRESSUS (Atlas daisy)	•					•		•			•	•			•		•			•		•		
ANDROSACE SARMENTOSA (rock jasmine)	•					•	•		•		•	•					•		•			•		
ANEMONE NEMOROSA (European wood anemone)		•			•	•	•	•			•	•			•		•	•	•			•		
ANEMONE PULSATILLA (European pasque flower)		•			•	•		•			•	•		•			•	•	•				•	
ANEMONELLA THALICTROIDES (rue anemone)	•	•				•		•			•	•			•		•		•			•		
AQUILEGIA FLABELLATA (fan columbine)		•	•			•		•			•	•			•		•	•	•			•	•	
ARABIS ALBIDA (wall rock cress)		•				•	•	•			•	•			•				•			•		
ARCTOSTAPHYLOS UVA-URSI (bearberry)		•				•	•			•	•	•	•	•	•					•		•		
ARENARIA MONTANA (mountain sandwort)	•					•	•		•		•	•			•	•				•		•	•	
ARISAEMA DRACONTIUM (green dragon)			•		•	•		•			•	•	•	•	•					•		•		
ARMERIA MARITIMA (common thrift)		•				•	•	•	•		•		•		•		•		•	•		•	•	
ARTEMISIA SCHMIDTIANA 'SILVER MOUND' (silver mound artemisia)		•				•	•	•			•	•			•					•		•	•	
ASARUM EUROPAEUM (European wild ginger)		•			•	•		•			•	•	•		•		•		•			•		
ASPERULA ODORATA (sweet woodruff)		•				•	•				•	•			•				•	•		•		
ASTER ALPINUS (alpine aster)		•				•	•	•	•		•				•		•	•	•	•	•	•	•	
AUBRIETA DELTOIDEA (purple rock cress)	•	•				•	•		•		•		•				•	•	•			•	•	
BELLIS PERENNIS (English daisy)	•					•	•	•			•				•		•		•	•		•	•	
BRUCKENTHALIA SPICULIFOLIA (spike heath)		•				•	•	•	•		•	•	•				•			•		•		
BUXUS MICROPHYLLA 'COMPACTA' (Kingsville dwarf boxwood)		•				•	•	•				•	•							•		•		
CALLIRHOE INVOLUCRATA (low poppy mallow)	•						•		•	•	•					•	•	•	•	•		•		
CALLUNA VULGARIS (Scotch heather)	•	•	•				•	•			•		•		•		•	•		•		•		
CAMPANULA CARPATICA (Carpathian harebell)		•				•	•	•			•		•					•	•	•	•	•	•	
CERATOSTIGMA PLUMBAGINOIDES (leadwort)		•				•	•	•	•		•	•						•		•	•	•		
CHAMAECYPARIS OBTUSA 'NANA GRACILIS' (Hinoki false cypress)			•			•	•	•					•							•				
CHRYSOGONUM VIRGINIANUM (goldenstar)		•				•	•	•			•					•			•	•		•		
CLAYTONIA VIRGINICA (Virginia spring beauty)		•				•	•	•			•	•		•			•		•			•		
CORYDALIS LUTEA (yellow corydalis)		•	•			•	•	•			•	•				•			•	•		•		•
CROCUS SATIVUS (saffron crocus)	•					•	•	•			•				•		•	•	•		•	•		
CROCUS VERSICOLOR (spring-flowering crocus)	•					•	•	•			•				•			•	•			•		
CRYPTOMERIA JAPONICA 'GLOBOSA NANA' (dwarf Japanese cedar)			•	•			•					•	•							•				
CYTISUS KEWENSIS (Kew broom)	•	•					•		•		•	•			•			•		•		•	•	•
DAPHNE CNEORUM (rose daphne)		•				•	•		•	•	•	•	•				•		•			•	•	
DICENTRA EXIMIA (fringed bleeding heart)			•			•	•	•			•	•			•		•		•	•	•	•	•	
DRABA MOLLISSIMA	•						•				•					•			•			•		
DRYAS OCTOPETALA (mountain avens)	•					•	•		•		•	•	•		•					•		•	•	
EDRAIANTHUS PUMILIO (grassy bells)	•						•		•		•						•	•	•			•	•	
EPIMEDIUM GRANDIFLORUM (bishop's hat)		•			•			•			•	•			•		•	•	•			•		
ERICA TETRALIX (cross-leaved heath)		•	•			•	•	•	•		•		•		•		•		•	•	•	•		
ERIGERON COMPOSITUS (fleabane)	•						•	•			•				•	•	•	•	•	•	•	•		
ERYTHRONIUM AMERICANUM (common fawn lily)	•	•				•		•			•					•			•			•		
ERYTHRONIUM DENS-CANIS (dog-tooth violet)		•				•		•			•				•		•	•	•			•		
GALAX APHYLLA (galax)		•			•	•			•		•	•	•		•				•	•		•		
GENTIANA ACAULIS (stemless gentian)	•					•	•	•			•							•	•	•		•		
GERANIUM SANGUINEUM (crane's-bill)			•			•	•	•			•	•					•			•		•		
GEUM REPTANS (avens)	•						•		•		•	•				•			•	•		•		
GYPSOPHILA REPENS 'FRATENSIS' (creeping babies'-breath)	•					•	•		•		•				•					•		•		

152

	PLANT HEIGHT				LIGHT NEEDS			GROWTH HABIT			SPECIAL TRAITS				FLOWER COLOR				FLOWER SEASON			SOIL NEEDS		
	Under 6 inches	6 to 12 inches	1 to 3 feet	Over 3 feet	Shade	Partial shade	Full sun	Upright	Spreading	Trailing	Flowers	Distinctive foliage	Evergreen	Decorative fruit	White to green	Yellow to orange	Pink to red	Blue to purple	Spring	Summer	Fall	Acid	Neutral	Alkaline
HELIANTHEMUM NUMMULARIUM (sun rose)		●				●	●	●	●	●	●	●	●			●	●		●	●			●	●
HEPATICA AMERICANA (hepatica)	●					●			●		●	●			●	●	●		●				●	
HUTCHINSIA ALPINA (alpencress)	●					●	●		●		●	●			●				●	●		●	●	
HYPERICUM CALYCINUM (Aaronsbeard St.-John's-wort)			●			●	●		●		●		●			●			●	●	●	●		
IBERIS SEMPERVIRENS 'SNOWFLAKE' (evergreen candytuft)		●				●	●		●		●		●		●				●				●	
ILEX CRENATA 'DWARF PAGODA' (Japanese holly)		●				●	●	●				●	●										●	
IRIS VERNA (vernal iris)	●	●				●	●		●		●	●						●	●			●		
JEFFERSONIA DIPHYLLA (American twinleaf)		●				●			●		●				●				●				●	
LEONTOPODIUM ALPINUM (edelweiss)		●					●		●		●				●					●			●	●
LEWISIA REDIVIVA (bitter-root)	●						●		●		●				●		●		●			●		
MITCHELLA REPENS (partridgeberry)	●				●	●				●	●		●	●	●		●		●			●		
MUSCARI BOTRYOIDES (common grape hyacinth)		●					●		●		●							●	●				●	●
OENOTHERA MISSOURENSIS (Ozark sundrops)		●					●		●	●	●					●				●	●			●
OMPHALODES VERNA (blue-eyed Mary)	●				●	●	●		●		●							●	●				●	
PHLOX SUBULATA (moss pink)	●					●	●		●		●				●		●	●	●				●	
PICEA GLAUCA 'CONICA' (dwarf Alberta spruce)			●			●	●	●				●	●										●	
POTENTILLA TRIDENTATA (three-toothed cinquefoil)		●					●		●	●	●				●				●			●		
PRIMULA AURICULA (auricula primrose)		●				●			●		●					●	●	●	●				●	●
PRIMULA DENTICULATA (Himalayan primrose)		●				●			●		●						●	●	●				●	
PRIMULA VERIS (cowslip)		●				●			●		●				●	●	●		●				●	
RANUNCULUS MONTANUS (mountain buttercup)	●					●	●		●		●					●			●				●	
RHODODENDRON 'DORA AMATEIS' (dwarf rhododendron)			●			●		●			●		●		●				●	●		●		
RHODODENDRON KEISKEI 'DWARF' (dwarf Keisk rhododendron)		●				●		●			●		●			●			●			●		
SAPONARIA OCYMOIDES (rock soapwort)		●					●		●	●	●						●		●	●			●	
SAXIFRAGA COTYLEDON (jungfrau saxifrage)		●				●	●		●		●				●					●			●	●
SAXIFRAGA KABSCHIA 'FERDINANDI-COBURGI' (saxifrage)	●					●			●		●		●			●			●				●	●
SEDUM RUPESTRE		●				●	●	●	●	●	●	●	●			●				●			●	●
SEDUM SIEBOLDII (October plant)		●				●	●		●	●	●	●					●				●		●	●
SEMPERVIVUM TECTORUM (common houseleek)		●				●	●		●		●	●	●				●			●			●	●
SILINE SCHAFTA (Schafta campion)	●					●	●		●		●						●	●		●	●		●	
TRILLIUM ERECTUM (purple trillium)		●	●		●	●		●			●				●	●	●		●			●		
TSUGA CANADENSIS 'COLE' (dwarf Canadian hemlock)	●					●	●		●	●		●	●										●	

Picture credits

The sources for the illustrations in this book are listed below. Credits from left to right are separated by semicolons, from top to bottom by dashes. Cover: Tom Tracy. 4: Sarah Tanner. 6: Tom Tracy. 8: Joseph A. Rosen, courtesy Hunt Institute for Botanical Documentation, Carnegie-Mellon University. 9: Derek Bayes, from *The Gardner's Chronicle,* January 1885, courtesy Lindley Library, Royal Horticultural Society, London. 11: Patrick Thurston. 12, 13: Patrick Thurston, except top left, courtesy Royal Horticultural Society, Wisley. 14: Courtesy U.S. National Agricultural Library. 18: John Neubauer. 23: Drawings by Kathy Rebeiz. 25-28: Tom Tracy. 30-33: Drawings by Kathy Rebeiz. 34: Sonja Bullaty and Angelo Lomeo. 35: John Neubauer—Pamela Harper. 37-41: Drawings by Kathy Rebeiz. 43: Tom Tracy. 44, 45: Pamela Harper—Tom Tracy. 46, 47: John Neubauer. 48, 49: Pamela Harper; Sonja Bullaty and Angelo Lomeo. 50, 51: Kim Steele.

52: Tom Tracy. 54, 56: Drawings by Kathy Rebeiz. 57: Bozidar Berginc. 59, 61: Drawings by Kathy Rebeiz. 65: Frank Lerner, courtesy Oriental Division, The New York Public Library, Astor, Lenox and Tilden Foundations. 66, 67: Courtesy Harvard University Library; John Neubauer. 68: John Neubauer. 69: From *The Alhambra* by Washington Irving; Richard Jeffery. 70, 71: John Neubauer. 72, 73: Kim Steele; Tom Tracy, top, from *Landscape Gardening in Japan* by Josiah Conder. 74: Henry Groskinsky. 77, 79: Drawings by Kathy Rebeiz. 81, 82: Henry Groskinsky. 83: Tom Tracy, except bottom right, Augie Salbosa. 84: R. Wagner, courtesy Van Ness Water Gardens. 88: Drawings by Kathy Rebeiz. 90: Illustration by Richard Crist. 92-149: Artists for encyclopedia illustrations listed in alphabetical order: Richard Crist, Susan M. Johnston, Mary Kellner, Gwen Leighton, Trudy Nicholson, Allianora Rosse. 150, 151: Maps by Adolph E. Brotman.

Characteristics of 22 bog and water plants

Listed below for quick reference are the species illustrated in Chapter 5.

	PLANT TYPE		GROWTH HABIT		SPECIAL TRAITS			WATER TEMP.				WATER DEPTH					PLANT HEIGHT			FLOWER COLOR						
	Bog	Aquatic	Floating	Upright	Flowers	Distinctive foliage	Evergreen	Under 32°	32° to 70°	Over 70°	Moist bog conditions	1 to 6 inches	6 to 12 inches	Under 1 foot	1 to 3 feet	Over 3 feet	White to green	Yellow to orange	Pink to red	Blue to purple	Multicolor	Spring	Summer	Fall
APONOGETON DISTACHYUS (Cape pondweed)		●	●		●	●	●		●			●			●		●						●	●
CALLA PALUSTRIS (water arum)	●	●		●	●				●	●		●			●		●						●	
CALTHA PALUSTRIS (marsh marigold)	●			●	●			●			●	●		●				●			●	●		
CANNA 'EREBUS' (aquatic canna)		●		●	●				●					●		●			●				●	●
CYPERUS ALTERNIFOLIUS (umbrella plant)	●	●		●		●			●		●			●		●	●						●	●
DROSERA ROTUNDIFOLIA (roundleaf sundew)	●			●	●	●		●			●	●							●				●	
EICHHORNIA CRASSIPES (water hyacinth)		●	●		●	●				●		●		●						●			●	
GENTIANA ANDREWSII (Andrews gentian)	●			●	●			●				●			●					●			●	
HYDROCLEYS NYMPHOIDES (water poppy)		●		●	●				●		●				●			●					●	●
IRIS KAEMPFERI 'KAGARI BI' (Japanese iris)	●			●	●			●				●			●					●			●	
LOBELIA CARDINALIS (cardinal flower)	●			●	●			●				●			●				●				●	●
NELUMBO NUCIFERA (sacred lotus)		●	●		●	●			●			●		●					●				●	
NYMPHAEA 'ATTRACTION' (attraction waterlily)		●	●		●			●	●			●	●						●				●	
NYMPHAEA COLORATA 'DIRECTOR GEORGE T. MOORE' (George T. Moore waterlily)		●	●		●				●	●		●	●							●			●	●
NYMPHAEA 'COMANCHE' (Comanche waterlily)		●	●		●				●	●		●	●								●		●	●
NYMPHAEA 'EMILY GRANT HUTCHINGS' (Emily Grant Hutchings waterlily)		●	●		●		●			●		●	●						●				●	●
PISTIA STRATIOTES (water lettuce)		●	●			●				●	●	●											●	
PONTEDERIA CORDATA (pickerel weed)	●	●		●	●			●		●		●		●					●				●	●
PRIMULA JAPONICA (Japanese primrose)	●			●	●			●				●			●				●			●	●	
SAGITTARIA SAGITTIFOLIA (Old World arrowhead)		●		●	●			●			●		●		●								●	
TROLLIUS LAXUS (spreading globeflower)	●			●	●			●				●		●			●					●		
TYPHA ANGUSTIFOLIA (narrow-leaved cattail)	●			●	●	●			●			●			●						●			●

Acknowledgments

The index for this book was prepared by Anita R. Beckerman. For their help in preparation of this book, the editors wish to thank the following: Dr. Robert J. Armstrong, Kennett Square, Pa.; Ernesta D. and Frederic L. Ballard, Chestnut Hill, Pa.; Morris Berd, Media, Pa.; Bozidar Berginc, West Allis, Wis.; Greg Boop, San Anselmo, Calif.; Dr. Alexej B. Borkovec, Silver Spring, Md.; Eleanor Brinckerhoff, Oliver Nurseries, Fairfield, Conn.; Jesse Brown, National Agricultural Library, Beltsville, Md.; Mr. and Mrs. Francis H. Cabot, Stonecrop Nurseries, Carmel, N.Y.; Mr. and Mrs. T. Emmott Chase, Orting, Wash.; Dr. Horace Clay, Honolulu, Hawaii; Roy Davidson, Seattle, Wash.; Mr. and Mrs. Richard Dresel, Greenbrae, Calif.; Don and Felicity Drukey, Format Design, Malibu, Calif.; Edwin Eberman, New Canaan, Conn.; Harold Epstein, Larchmont, N.Y.; Mrs. Robert C. Erb, New Canaan, Conn.; Mrs. Sara Faust, Stonecrop Nurseries, Carmel, N.Y.; Ms. Nora Fields, New York Botanical Gardens, Bronx, N.Y.; Marion M. Flook, Wilmington, Del.; Roxie E. Gevjan, Newton Square, Pa.; Harold Greer, Greer Gardens, Eugene, Ore.; Harland Hand, El Cerrito, Calif.; Pamela Harper, Seaford, Va.; Mrs. John S. Kistler, West Chester, Pa.; Don Korsmo, Seattle, Wash.; Mr. and Mrs. Robert Edmund Lee, Washington, D.C.; Eloise Lesan, Cos Cob, Conn.; Jane Liu, Cos Cob, Conn.; Professor MacDougall, Dumbarton Oaks Garden Library, Washington, D.C.; James A. Minogue, American Rock Garden Society, Bentonville, Va.; Elizabeth A. Mosimann, Assistant Librarian, Hunt Botanical Library, Carnegie-Mellon University, Pittsburgh, Pa.; Oehme, Van Sweden and Associates, Inc., Washington, D.C.; John P. Osborne, Westport, Conn.; James Pendleton, Good Earth Nursery, Burke, Va.; William Platt, Platt, Wyckoff & Coles, Architects, New York, N.Y.; Dr. Gordon Pollock, New Canaan, Conn.; Robert Scace, Librarian, Royal Horticultural Society, Wisley, England; George Schenk, Bothell, Wash.; Bruce Schmidlin, William Tricker, Inc., Saddle River, N.J.; Carol Ruth Shepherd, New Canaan, Conn.; Mrs. Walter Simpson, Director, Longue Vue Gardens, New Orleans, La.; Joel W. Spingann, Baldwin, N.Y.; Edith Stern, Longue Vue Gardens, New Orleans, La.; Martin Stoelzel, San Rafael, Calif.; Powers Taylor, Rosedale Nurseries, Hawthorne, N.Y.; Charles B. Thomas, Lilypons Water Gardens, Lilypons, Md.; Bill and Carol Uber, Van Ness Water Gardens, Upland, Calif.; Mr. and Mrs. Leo Vollmer, Baltimore, Md.; Eulalie M. Wagner, Tacoma, Wash.; Dr. Richard Wagner, Torrence, Calif; John Warwick, Superintendent of the Rock Garden, Royal Horticultural Society, Wisley, England; Olga Wolhaupter, Los Angeles, Calif.; John A. Wood, El Rancho Tropi-Cal, Thermal, Calif.; Madeline Zilfi, Professor of Middle Eastern Studies, University of Maryland, College Park, Md.

Bibliography

Allan, Mea, *Plants That Changed Our Gardens*. David & Charles, London, 1974.

Anderson, Alice S., *Our Garden Heritage*. Dodd, Mead & Co., 1961.

Ashberry, Anne, *Miniature Gardens*. D. Van Nostrand Company, Inc., 1952.

Bartrum, Douglas, *Water in the Garden*. John Gifford Limited, London, 1968.

Berrall, Julia S., *The Garden: An Illustrated History*. The Viking Press, 1966.

Birdseye, Clarence and Eleanor, *Growing Woodland Plants*. Oxford Univ. Press, Inc., 1951.

Bohm, Cestmir, *Rock Garden Plants*. The Hamlyn Publishing Group, Inc., 1970.

Brooklyn Botanic Garden, *Dwarf Conifers*. BBG, 1973.

Brooklyn Botanic Garden, *Handbook on Miniature Gardens*. BBG, 1976.

Brooklyn Botanic Garden, *Handbook on Rock Gardens*. BBG, 1973.

Brooklyn Botanic Garden, *Rhododendrons and Their Relatives*. BBG, 1971.

Calkins, Carroll, *Gardening with Water, Plantings and Stone*. Walker & Co., 1974.

Chittenden, Fred J., ed., *The Royal Horticultural Society Dictionary of Gardening*, 2nd Ed. Clarendon Press, 1974.

Clifford, Derek, *A History of Garden Design*. Praeger Publishers, 1963.

Coats, Peter, *Great Gardens of the Western World*. G. P. Putnam's Sons, 1963.

Cox, E. H. M., *Farrer's Last Journey*. Dunlau & Co. Ltd., London, 1926.

Cuthbert, *Guide to Growing Rock Plants*. Cassell & Co. Ltd., London, 1953.

Dulta, Reginald, *Water Gardening Indoors and Out*. Crown Publishers, Inc., 1977.

Edwards, Alexander, *Rock Gardens*. Abelard-Schuman Limited, 1958.

Eliovson, Sima, *Gardening the Japanese Way*. Howard Timmins, 1970.

Elliot, Roy, *Alpine Gardening*. Vista, London, 1963.

Farrer, Reginald, *The English Rock Garden*. Theophrastus, Sakonnet, R.I., 1928.

Farrer, Reginald, *My Rock Garden*. Theophrastus, Sakonnet, R.I., 1945.

Farrer, Reginald, *The Rainbow Bridge*. Edward Arnold & Co., London, 1921.

Foster, H. Lincoln, *Rock Gardening*. Houghton Mifflin Co., 1968.

Griffith, Anna N., *A Guide to Rock Garden Plants*. E. P. Dutton & Co., Inc., 1965.

Gwynn, Stephen, *Claude Monet and his Garden*. The Macmillan Company, 1934.

Healey, B. J., *The Plant Hunters*. Charles Scribner's Sons, 1975.

Heath, Royton E., *Miniature Rock Gardening in Troughs and Pans*. W. H. & L. Collingridge, Ltd., London, 1957.

Heath, Royton E., *Rock Plants for Small Gardens*. Collingridge Books, 1969.

Heritage, Bill, *Water Gardening*. Hamlyn, 1973.

Hills, Lawrence D., *Alpines Without a Garden*. Faber & Faber Limited, London, 1953.

Hills, Lawrence D., *Miniature Alpine Gardening*. Faber & Faber Limited, London, 1945.

Hornibrook, Murray, *Dwarf and Slow-Growing Conifers*. Country Life Ltd., 1923.

Huxley, Anthony, *An Illustrated History of Gardening*. Paddington Press Ltd., 1978.

Huxley, Anthony and Alan R. Toogood, *Garden Perennials and Water Plants*. Macmillan Publishing Co., Inc., 1970.

Ingwerson, Will, *Ingwerson's Manual of Alpine Plants*. Will Ingwerson and Dunsprint Ltd., 1978.

Jekyll, Gertrude, *Wall and Water Gardens*. Charles Scribner's Sons, 1901.

Jellicoe, Susan and Geoffrey, *Water: The Use of Water in Landscape Architecture*. St. Martin's Press, Inc., 1971.

Kolaga, Walter A., *All About Rock Gardens and Plants*. Doubleday & Company, Inc., 1966.

Kramer, Jack, *Water Gardening: Pools, Fountains and Plants*. Charles Scribner's Sons, 1971.

Krutch, Joseph Wood, *The Gardener's World*. G. P. Putnam's Sons, 1959.

Macself, A. J., *Simple Rock Gardening*. W. H. & L. Collingridge Limited, London, 1949.

Masters, Charles O., *Encyclopedia of the Water-lily*. T. F. H. Publications, Inc. Ltd., 1974.

Miles, Bebe, *Bluebells and Bittersweet: Gardening with Native American Plants*. Van Nostrand Reinhold Company, 1969.

Perry, Frances, *The Garden Pool*. Great Albion Books, 1972.

Perry, Frances, *Water Gardening*. Country Life, 1938.

Proudley, Brian and Valerie, *Heathers in Color*. Hippocrene Books, Inc., 1974.

Puttock, A. G., *Rock Gardening*. Magna Print Books, Litton, Yorkshire, 1975.

Reader's Digest Association, Ltd., *Reader's Digest Encyclopaedia of Garden Plants and Flowers*. RDA, Ltd., 1971.

Rickett, H. W., *Wild Flowers of the United States*. McGraw-Hill Book Co., 1975.

Robinson, William, *The English Flower Garden*. John Murray, London, 1956.

Rockwell, F. F., *Rock Gardens*. The Macmillan Company, 1928.

Sanders, T. W., *Rock Gardens and Alpine Plants*. W. H. & L. Collingridge, London, 1922.

Schenk, George, *Rock Gardens*. Lane Book Company, 1970.

Schimper, A. F. W., *Plant-Geography*. Hafner Publishing Co., 1960.

Shewell-Cooper, W. E., ed., *Alpine & Rock Gardening*. Seeley Service & Co. Limited, London, 1961.

Shewell-Cooper, W. E., *Rock Gardens and Pools*. Drake Publishers Inc., 1973.

Skinner, Henry T., *The Rock Garden*. N.Y. State College of Agriculture at Cornell, 1977.

Staff of the L. H. Bailey Hortorium, Cornell University, *Hortus Third: A Dictionary of Plants Cultivated in the United States and Canada*. Macmillan Publishing Co., Inc., 1976.

Stark, Francis B. and Conrad B. Link, *Rock Gardens and Water Plants in Color*. Doubleday & Company, Inc., 1973.

Stetson, Paul, *Garden Pools*. T. F. H. Publications, Inc., 1963.

Stodola, Dr. Jiri, *Encyclopedia of Water Plants*. T. F. H. Publications, Inc., 1967.

Sunset Editors, *Garden Pools, Fountains and Waterfalls*. Lane Publishing Co., 1974.

Swindells, Philip, *Water Gardening*. Charles Scribner's Sons, 1975.

Symons-Jeune, B. H. B., *Natural Rock Gardening*. Charles Scribner's Sons, 1933.

Taylor, N., ed., *Encyclopedia of Gardening*, 4th ed. Houghton Mifflin Company, 1961.

Thomas, Dr. G. L., Jr., *Goldfish Pools, Water-lilies and Tropical Fishes*. T. F. H. Publications, Inc., 1965.

Thomas, H. H., *Rock Gardening for Amateurs*. Cassell & Co. Ltd., London, 1926.

Thornton, Archie, *Rock Garden Primer*. A. T. DeLaMare Company, Inc., 1931.

Underhill, Terry, *Heaths and Heathers*. Drake Publishers, Inc., 1972.

Vivian, John, *Building Stone Walls*. Garden Way Publishing, 1978.

Whittle, Tyler, *The Plant Hunters*. Chilton Book Co., 1970.

Wilder, Louise Beebe, *Pleasures and Problems of a Rock Garden*. Garden City Publishing Company, Inc., 1928.

Wilder, Louise B., *The Rock Garden*. Doubleday & Company, Inc., 1935.

Wright, Richardson, *The Story of Gardening*. Garden City Publishing Company, Inc., 1938.

Wyman, Donald, *Wyman's Gardening Encyclopedia*. Macmillan Publishing Co., Inc., 1977.

Index

PRINTED IN U.S.A.